Automation in
Commercial Banking

GRADUATE SCHOOL OF BUSINESS DISSERTATIONS SERIES,
Columbia University and The Free Press

L. R. Burgess, *Top Executive Pay Package*
P. O. Dietz, *Pension Funds: Measuring Investment Performance*
T. C. Gaines, *Techniques of Treasury Debt Management*
B. Yavitz, *Automation in Commercial Banking: Its Process and Impact*

Automation in Commercial Banking

Its Process and Impact

*A CASE STUDY
AND CONCEPTUAL ANALYSIS*

by BORIS YAVITZ

*A Joint Publication of
The Graduate School of Business,
Columbia University, and
The Free Press*

Collier-Macmillan Canada, Ltd., Toronto, Ontario

Library of Congress Catalog Card Number 67–12521

First Printing

To My Parents
Simon and Miriam Yavitz

1402198

Preface

Bank automation is a relatively recent phenomenon, still in its early stages of development. The first electronic computers made their earliest appearance in commercial banking only a few years ago. Their real penetration of the industry can be properly dated as recently as 1960 or 1961.

In dealing with a topic so recent in origin and one subject to so rapid a rate of obsolescence of current data, it becomes essential to supplement information from published sources with direct personal contact in the field. The writer has been fortunate in eliciting the necessary help and cooperation from many people knowledgeable and active in bank automation.

The kind assistance of Booz, Allen & Hamilton, Inc., the American Bankers Association, and the many individuals in both organizations who gave of their time and effort is gratefully acknowledged. An equal debt of gratitude is due to the several banks and their officers who shared their experiences and opinions with the writer. Individual acknowledgement, by name, is precluded by their very number and to prevent the direct identification of bank experiences cited under fictitious names.

The writer also wishes to acknowledge the contribution of the members of his dissertation Advisory Committee, Professors Eli Ginzberg (Chairman), Roger F. Murray, and Charles E. Summer, Jr. Their help, guidance, patience, and understanding have been invaluable.

Finally, and closer to home, my heartfelt thanks to my wife, Irene, for many hours of typing, proofreading, and checking, and my daughters, Jessica, Judy, and Emily, for maintaining the peace while "Daddy did his homework."

BORIS YAVITZ

ASSOCIATE PROFESSOR OF BUSINESS
GRADUATE SCHOOL OF BUSINESS
COLUMBIA UNIVERSITY

Contents

Preface   vii

List of Tables   xii

List of Illustrations   xiv

I
Introduction   1

II
Commercial Banking Adopts the Computer—Economic, Institutional, and Technological Parameters

    6

2.1. *Commercial Banking in a World of Change —Economic and Institutional Factors*   7

2.2. *Electronic Computers Come of Age—The Technological Advances*   17

2.3. *The Banking System's Preparation for Computer Adoption* 21

2.4. *The Rapid Proliferation of Computer Technology* 28

III
The Individual Bank's Decision to Automate 31

3.1. *Typical Steps in the Decision To Automate* 32

3.2. *Economic and Technical Focus of the Decision to Automate* 35

3.3. *The Economics of Bank Automation—Cost Versus Savings* 40

3.4. *Aids to Proliferation—A Comparative Case Study: Pioneer Versus New Recruit* 47

3.5. *Some Obstacles to Proliferation of Bank Automation* 54

IV
Diversified Computer Applications— A Broad Range of Options 61

4.1. *Principal Factors in the Diversification of Computer Applications* 63

4.2. *An Overview of the Diversification of Computer Applications* 66

4.3. *Pricing of External Services* 72

4.4. *Marketing of External Services* 74

V
The Process of Automation— A Conceptual View 77

5.1. *Graphic Representation of Computer Applications* 83

5.2.   The Concept of the Exploitation-Path   85
5.3.   The Determinants of a Firm's Exploitation-
        Path   89
5.4.   A Relatively Unique Set of Determinants   102

VI

Contrasts in Automation—
Four Case Experiences   106

6.1.   Essex County National Bank   107
6.2.   Manufacturers National Bank   113
6.3.   Metropolitan Bank and Trust Company   117
6.4.   Fidelity Bank and Trust Company   124

VII

The Impacts of Automation—
Empirical and Theoretical   130

7.1.   Impacts on Employment   131
7.2.   Organizational Structure   137
7.3.   Managerial Functions   141
7.4.   Banking Services   143
7.5.   The Impacts of Automation—An Oversim-
        plification   145

VIII

Implications   150

8.1.   Summary and Conclusions   150
8.2.   Emerging Implications   154

Bibliography   162

Index   165

List of Tables

2.1 Increasing Competition from Nonbank Financial
    Institutions, 1946–1962   8

2.2 Shifting Composition of Commercial Bank Deposits:
    Increasing Ratio of Savings and Time Deposits to
    Demand Deposits   9

2.3 Projected Volumes of Commercial Bank Activity,
    1960–1975   11

2.4 Consolidations and Branching: Fewer Banks,
    More Branches   12

2.5 Insured Commercial Banks and Their Deposits
    Distributed by Bank Size   30

3.1 "Reasons for Our Decision to Automate"—Survey
    Responses of 697 Banks   37

3.2 "Internal Applications Status" in Deposit and Loan
    Accounting—Survey Responses of 348 Banks   38

3.3 Applications to Be Installed by Banks Planning
    Automation   39

3.4   Initial Computer Applications in 40 Commercial
        Banks   40
3.5   Summarized Data for 20 Banks from Feasibility
        Studies by Booz, Allen & Hamilton   44
3.6   Summarized Data for 19 Banks Operating
        Cooperative Center from Feasibility Studies by
        Booz, Allen & Hamilton   45

List of Illustrations

2.1   Average Weekly Gross Earnings of Non-Supervisory
      Workers in Banking in the United States, 1947–64   14
2.2   Standard Check with MICR-Coding and Fields   26
5.1   Graphic Representation of Two Computer
      Applications   84
5.2   Successive Applications in a Bank's Automation
      Program   86
5.3   The Exploitation-Path   88
6.1   Exploitation-Path: Essex County National Bank   109
6.2   Exploitation-Path: Manufacturers National Bank   114
6.3   Exploitation-Path: Metropolitan Bank and Trust
      Company   123
6.4   Exploitation-Path: Fidelity Bank and Trust
      Company   128

I

Introduction

Automation and its impacts are probably among the most widely discussed topics in business literature today. Whether the discussion is scholarly or popular, it is characterized by lively interest and a broad range of controversy.

Will automation bring about a level of unemployment to rival the depths of the Great Depression, or will it herald a new era of labor shortage? Will it result in a total regimentation and dehumanizing of the corporate employee, or will it liberate him from the grinding monotony of repetitive work to challenge his creative and intellectual capabilities? Will it produce more—or less—centralization of management; more—or less—responsibility and job satisfaction for the corporate manager?

This study—let it be stated at the outset—does not purport to provide the definitive answers to these questions. Rather, it is an attempt to develop some structure within which these problems may be meaningfully analyzed and understood. It seeks to evolve a conceptual scheme, or model, from the empirical evidence of a case history of automation.

Automation in the commercial banking system was selected for investigation. Commercial banking has the distinct advantage of being a narrowly defined industry with a high order of homogeneity. Automation, as applied to bank operations, is equally well-defined and homogeneous. It is centered on stock models of commercially available, general-purpose digital computers.

This electronic hardware has the further advantage of being recognized as "automation," by almost any definition—popular or technical.[1]

Early in the work it became clear that a broad, industry-wide view was essential but that it had to be supplemented by some individual company data and experience. In order to obtain sufficiently broad coverage of bank automation, a variety of data sources was used.

On the individual-firm level:

1. The author interviewed the bank officers of eight banks and made a comprehensive inspection of their computer operations.

2. The author enlisted the help and cooperation of Booz, Allen & Hamilton, Inc. This management consulting firm, generally thought to be the most experienced in the field of bank automation, made available the data gathered in its automation-feasibility studies for forty commercial bank clients.

On the industry-wide level:

3. Through the kind cooperation of the automation division of the American Bankers Association, the writer was given full access to questionnaire responses to its Automation Survey, conducted in September 1963. A total of 3,990 banks responded to this nationwide survey. Only a portion of its results had been published by the ABA in 1964 at the time of writing.

4. Also with the cooperation of the ABA, the writer attended its National Automation Conference (Chicago, November 1963) and participated in all its working study groups. This was the first national conference ever assembled to discuss automation in banking, and was attended by over 1,200 bankers. Its speakers and discussion leaders represented the leading authorities, in their respective topics, according to the industry's own evaluation.

On the intermediate level:

---

1. James R. Bright, *Automation and Management* (Boston: Harvard University Press, 1958), Appendix I.

2

5. The writer interviewed some twenty bankers at the National Automation Conference. They were questioned at various lengths and on a variety of topics. The main interest was in detecting whether any regional differences existed, as a balance to the intensive interviewing confined to banks in the northeastern states.

6. The author obtained valuable information from interviews with several consultants on the Booz, Allen & Hamilton staff who discussed their experiences with more than fifty bank-automation programs. Similarly, officers of ABA's automation and marketing divisions were interviewed, and their views of industry-wide developments were solicited.

A brief outline of the topics dealt with, in each of the following chapters, will serve to clarify our approach and the organization of our material.

Chapter II. We have examined the historical and environmental parameters within which the commercial banking system adopted the electronic computer. The focus is industry-wide, and the economic, institutional, and technological determinants that brought automation to banking are traced. The presentation is both descriptive and analytic. We not only relate what happened, but also attempt to show why and how it happened.

Chapter III. Shifting the focus to the individual bank, we have examined the decision to automate. The effects of the same economic and technological determinants on the individual firm are considered. The highly economic orientation of the decision to automate is noted, and its dollar-and-cents content is analyzed. A quantitative analysis of the cost-versus-returns calculus for twenty automated banks is presented. Two brief case histories point up the extent to which the road to automation has been rendered safe and relatively painless in a few short years of experience.

Chapter IV. We have examined the wide range of options that automation presents to the individual bank. In almost every case, automation is first applied to check handling and demand-deposit accounting. We soon see, however, that a series of economic, technological, and human factors combine to spur each bank into adding to, and elaborating on, its repertoire of computer applications. The range of such applications is almost unlimited. In this chapter there is an overview of several types of applications selected by a variety of banks, as some indication of the diversity of available options.

Chapter V. We have developed a conceptual framework, tying together the empirical evidence presented in the preceding chapters. Without some framework, the process of automation, as represented by bank automation, appears no more than a confusing patchwork of empirical observations. Our model views the process of automation as the progressive exploitation of a bundle of capabilities opened up by a technological advance. These capabilities are viewed along three analytical axes, which are closely related to the operational objectives of a profit-seeking firm. Within this three-dimensional space, we can trace an "exploitation-path" to represent the dynamic process of automation within each firm. Using the case history examined, we can identify a series of determinants shaping and forming this path. The effect of such variables as competition, technical characteristics of hardware, bank size and location are considered in turn. We conclude that a relatively unique set of determinants confronts each automating bank. The result is a great variety of exploitation-path shapes, probably classifiable in a number of typological categories.

Chapter VI. This chapter illustrates by actual case histories some of the exploitation-path patterns evident to date. Case histories of four banks are presented, their exploitation-paths are plotted, and their differences and similarities are contrasted. The four banks were selected to present as wide a contrast as possible. Each significant difference in the use of automation is related to each bank's exploitation-path. Some of the impacts on each bank are also briefly noted.

Chapter VII. Here, we have tackled that most popular of topics, the impacts of automation. Such impacts are briefly considered in four major areas: employment, organizational struc-

4

ture, managerial functions, and banking services. It is noted that, despite extensive discussion of the computer revolution and the high-powered hardware already installed in many banks, dramatic impacts are generally conspicuous by their absence. By relating the impacts of automation to its process, as conceptually visualized in our model, the current absence of dramatic change becomes quite understandable. The same relationship explains why such impacts as are observable to date—both in the four selected cases and in the industry at large—indicate considerable variations between one bank and another.

Using these conclusions, we then examine the validity of the many generalizations and forecasts of the impacts of automation. It becomes quite clear that any generalization that views automation as a one-dimensional variable is grossly oversimplified and highly likely to prove unreliable. Similarly limited is any view that equates automation with its hardware. Both our case studies and the conceptual analysis strongly refute the assumptions implicit in these oversimplified views. Yet it is probably true that most sweeping predictions of the impacts of automation are grounded in these assumptions.

Chapter VIII. The final chapter is concerned with the implications of this study. We examine the applicability of these findings to a more general understanding of automation and discuss the usefulness of our model in relating impacts to process.

I I

Commercial Banking Adopts the Computer—Economic, Institutional and Technological Parameters

The adoption of the electronic computer by the commercial banking system represents a technological advance of significant magnitude. As James R. Bright has stated:

... technological advances are not made in economic, social and political vacuums. Technological progress often is paced or directed by non-technological forces, and sheer luck, change and the happy concurrence of genius and needs will sometimes alter progress enormously. It is absolutely essential to consider also the non-technological factors influencing technological efforts and directions.[1]

A clear analysis of the introduction of automation to bank operations and its subsequent proliferation therefore requires an understanding of the setting within which this process evolved. It will be seen that almost every nontechnological factor mentioned by Bright did indeed affect the course and direction of bank automation.

The history of and progress in computer technology are per-

---

1. James R. Bright, "Directions of Technological Change and Some Business Consequences," *Automation and Technological Change* (Columbus, Ohio: Battelle Memorial Institute, 1963), p. 10.

haps best viewed as first, the developments in banking that gave rise to the demand, and second, the advances in computer technology that provided the supply. Each of these will be reviewed in turn, the former in considerably greater detail than the latter.

2.1. Commercial Banking in a World of Change— Economic and Institutional Factors

The commercial banking system of the United States has, in recent years, been subjected to considerable pressures resulting from changing trends in business, financial, and social institutions. Although some of these trends may be traced back to the early 1930's, their major influence—for the purpose of this study—began to be felt in the years since World War II, and has been growing at an accelerating rate since. It should be emphasized that our main interest in tracing these trends is focused on the bank as a business enterprise rather than as a creator of money or a tool of monetary policy. In this frame of reference the banker, as a business manager, is interested in attracting deposits of various kinds and using them to yield a profit after paying for their use and covering the expense of all services rendered in connection with their acquisition and investment. While the profit-making objective is common to most business managers, the banker must pursue it within a more restrictive framework and subject to the constraints of several regulatory agencies having direct jurisdiction.[2] These agencies and the occasional conflicts between them have been instrumental in some reshaping of commercial bank operations. Other, more direct pressures have resulted from the changing practices of both individuals and corporations in their financial dealings.

Let us first look at the revenue side of bank operations and

---

2. These may include the Comptroller of the Currency, Federal Reserve Bank, Federal Deposit Insurance Corporation, Department of Justice, and the state banking commissions.

Table 2.1—Increasing Competition from Nonbank Financial Institutions, 1946–1962*

Year	SAVINGS AND LOAN ASSOCIATIONS		CREDIT UNIONS		MUTUAL SAVINGS BANKS		COMMERCIAL BANKS			
	Deposits (in billions)	Index	Deposits (in billions)	Index	Deposits (in billions)	Index	Savings and Time Deposits (in billions)	Index	Total Deposits (in billions)	Index
1946	$ 9	100	$½	100	$20	100	$ 40	100	$140	100
1954	40	444	2	400	30	150	50	125	170	122
1962	90	1000	6	1200	40	200	100	250	263	188

* Source: Federal Reserve Bulletin.

note briefly several trends that have made income production a more difficult task for the commercial banker.

With the growing financial sophistication of both individuals and corporate treasurers, commercial banks have been encountering progressively stiffer competition in attracting deposits and have, in fact, been losing ground to other financial institutions. Table 2.1 contrasts the rate of expansion of total commercial bank deposits between 1946 and 1962 with that of three other types of institutions. The 88 per cent growth for commercial banks is hardly impressive in contrast with competitors' growth records.

The growing competition for deposits has also adversely affected the *composition* of deposits held by commercial banks. Demand deposits—the traditional mainstay of commercial banks and their cheapest form of "raw material"—accounted for only 56 per cent of total deposits in 1963, as against 69 per cent in 1955. The much more costly sources of savings and time deposits have correspondingly increased from 31 per cent to 44 per cent of total deposits.

Table 2.2. clearly illustrates the trend in the changing composition of deposits, and contrasts the relative growth rates of demand deposits with that of savings and time deposits.

Table 2.2—Shifting Composition of Commercial Bank Deposits: Increasing Ratio of Savings and Time Deposits to Demand Deposits*

	TOTAL DEPOSITS	SAVINGS AND TIME DEPOSITS		DEMAND DEPOSITS		GROWTH INDICES		
Year	(Billion $)	(Billion $)	Per cent of Total	(Billion $)	Per cent of Total	Total Deposits	Savings and Time	Demand Deposits
1955	160	50	31	110	69	100	100	100
1957	170	55	32	115	68	106	110	105
1959	180	60	33	120	67	112	120	109
1961	202	77	38	125	62	126	154	114
1963	230	102	44	128	56	144	204	116

* Source: Federal Reserve Bulletin.

Short-term business loans have traditionally been a major source of bank income. In recent years, however, most large corporations have increased their ability to finance their working-capital requirements out of retained earnings, more liberal depreciation allowances, and improved cash flows. Many corporations have, in effect, entered the business-loan field themselves, either via direct intercompany lending or through the medium of commercial paper. As an indication of the magnitude of this trend, we find that during 1962 commercial banks increased their business loans by 7.7 per cent, but the total commercial paper outstanding rose 27 per cent over 1961.[3]

The restriction of commercial bank underwriting activities under the National Banking Act of 1933 has in recent years acted to depress bank earnings. Under the provisions of that act, banks could only underwrite Federal government, Federal agency, and tax-exempt general-obligation bonds of states and municipalities. The last category provided a substantial source of revenue to many commercial banks until the recent trend among states and municipalities to issue so-called revenue bonds. Prior to 1962, these bonds were considered prohibited to commercial bank underwriting, thus depriving them of an important source of income. Similar prohibitions—or, in some cases, lack of clear-cut authorizations—often prevented commercial banks from bolstering revenues by expansion into other than traditionally prescribed banking areas.

The four trends just cited have combined to curtail bank operating revenues and restrict the revenue-producing options open to commercial banks. It is not surprising that bank managements have been actively striving to alleviate these restrictions by a variety of responses.

In order to make up for the drop in corporate deposits, many banks aggressively went after the small, individual depositor. Special-checking accounts (requiring no minimum balance) and a friendly, welcome-to-the-public image were the chief avenues of attack. Most banks geared themselves to an all-out "retail" operation, offering a broad range of banking services in easily accessible branches designed to reach an ever-widening segment

---

3. "Banking Turmoil—Conflicts Beset Banks," *Wall Street Journal* (October 4, 1963), p. 1.

of the population. The trend has been called a "shift from class to mass banking."

This trend, supplemented by an increasing number of check payments by business and government, resulted in a dramatic rise in the volume of checks cleared annually through the commercial banking system. In 1939, banks processed approximately three and one-half billion checks. This volume increased to six and one-half billion by 1950 and to over thirteen billion by 1960. Therefore, in the decade of the 1950's the number of checks processed expanded by 75 per cent. During the same period the total value of demand deposits increased by only 37 per cent. If computed in *constant* dollars, total demand deposits actually represented a *decrease* of 2 per cent.

The spectacular rise in check volume and activity, with no corresponding increase in the value of deposits, placed a severe strain on the banking system. Substantially more paper had to be processed and, unless processing costs could be sharply reduced, profit margins on demand-deposit operations were seriously threatened. Nor did the decade of the 1960's promise any abatement in the trend. Bank activities for the period 1960–1975 are projected in Table 2.3.

Table 2.3—Projected Volumes of Commercial Bank Activity, 1960–1975*

Year	Number of Demand-Deposit Accounts	Average Checks Cleared per Account	Total Number of Checks Cleared (in billions)
1960	57,000,000	60	13
1965	66,000,000	67	17
1970	78,000,000	74	22
1975	92,000,000	81	29

* Source: Bureau of Labor Statistics, Monthly Labor Review, Vol. 85, No. 9.

A second, and more subtle, factor in the striking increase of paper work during this period has been the increased velocity of deposit turnover. Professor Paul S. Nadler has only recently pointed out this phenomenon in commercial bank deposits. In 1946 New York City banks turned over their deposits twenty-five times per annum; in 1962 turnover reached seventy-eight times per annum. For six other major centers turnover rose from eighteen to forty-one in the same period. Nadler notes:

> ... the increase in turnover of money means that each dollar of demand deposits on hand is churning more rapidly and causing the banks more work and expense of handling.

Thus turnover of money actually results in a double squeeze on the banks. First it limits the rise in demand deposits and thus the rise in earning assets based on demand deposit funds. In addition it forces the banks to do more work and incur more expense as the demand deposits the banks do have turn over more rapidly to finance more of the economy's activity.[4]

A corollary result of the shift to retail banking, with its rising costs, has been a two-pronged trend toward one, mergers, acquisitions, and consolidations of banks, and two, an impressive expansion in the number of branch offices. Between 1946 and 1962 there was a net drop of 779 in the number of commercial banks in the United States, coupled with an increase of 8,428 branches. As shown in Table 2.4, there has been a steady increase in the ratio of branches to banks, from .286 in 1946 to .928 in 1962.

Table 2.4—Consolidations and Branching: Fewer Banks, More Branches*

Year	Number of Banks	Number of Branches	Total Number of Bank Offices	Branches per Bank
1946	14,218	4,063	18,281	.286
1950	13,800	5,200	19,000	.377
1954	13,500	6,500	20,000	.480
1958	13,000	9,500	22,500	.730
1962	13,439	12,491	25,930	.928

* Derived from article and bar charts, Robert Sheehan, "What's Rocking Those Rocks, the Banks," *Fortune* (October 1963), pp. 110–111.

It should be noted that both mergers and branch expansions were achieved in the face of stringent constraints and restrictions by Federal and state regulatory authorities. There is little doubt that without such regulation the statistics of both categories would have been substantially higher.

---

4. Paul S. Nadler, "What Stunts the Growth of Demand Deposits?" *Banking* (January, 1964), p. 53.

In response to depositors' reluctance to maintain balances in non-income-producing demand-deposit accounts, commercial banks intensified their efforts to lure both savings and time deposits. The comparatively steeper rise in the savings and time deposits was indicated in Table 2.2.

The drive for savings and time deposits has certainly built up total deposits, but its effect on bank operating costs has already been noted. Although demand deposits are interest free, as much as 4 per cent interest has been paid by banks for saving and time deposits. The pressure on profit margins, as a result of this response, is substantial and self-evident.

In a similar response to make up for declining activity in business loans, most banks intensified their pursuit of consumer loans and, more recently, mortgage financing. Both these forms of lending, however, entail substantially higher administrative expense than commercial loans.

The keen competition for deposits between the commercial banking system and other financial institutions, as well as competition within the system, has forced banks to broaden the scope and extent of services offered to depositors. Many of these services have either been given free or charged off against offsetting balances. Although many bankers felt it was essential to offer such services, they were also keenly aware of the added cost, with the further encroachment on profit margins.

Bank operating costs have also been rising steadily as a result of the general increase in the level of wages and salaries, as well as the rising costs of all products and services. The increase in bank personnel costs alone is clearly illustrated in Figure 2.1, showing average weekly gross earnings of nonsupervisory employees in banking in the United States, between 1947 and 1964. Most consultants, based on their experience in the field, currently assume a 3 per cent annual increase in personnel costs when projecting bank operating costs.

Besides rising wage scales, the spectacular increase in check volume has placed a strain on the availability of competent clerical workers. This has been particularly noticeable in the repeti-

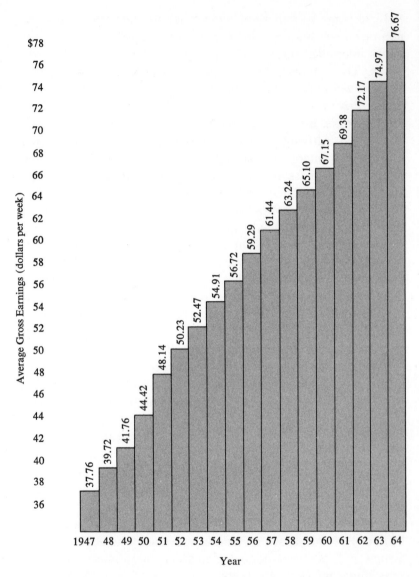

Figure 2.1—Average Weekly Gross Earnings of Nonsupervisory Workers in Banking in the United States, 1947–1964*

* *Source:* U.S. Department of Commerce, *Business Statistics,* The Biennial Supplement to the Survey of Current Business (1965).

14

tive and often tedious jobs found in check handling and book-keeping departments. These jobs are commonly staffed by women and have typically been subject to high turnover. Many banks report turnover rates in excess of 30 per cent—and often as high as 50 per cent. One bank president even cited 80 per cent turnover in some West Coast banks. The adverse effect on operating costs of turnover rates of this magnitude is self-evident.

Thus in the years since World War II commercial banks were faced with a serious threat to profit margins, as a result of the combined effect of the revenue-lowering and cost-increasing trends we have reviewed. It is not surprising, therefore, that while credit officers were busily pursuing new sources of income, operating officers were aggressively seeking new methods, techniques, and equipment that promised lower costs. The electronic computer, which first began to attract business interest in the mid-1950's, was seen as a potentially useful tool in the struggle for lower costs.

For the banking system as a whole, however, the computer—interestingly enough—was carried in on the coattails of its peripheral equipment. Most bankers were chiefly interested in a device for high-speed, mechanical handling of checks, an interest that led to the development of the sorter-reader. Inasmuch as this device had to be controlled by some form of electronic circuitry and bankers soon discovered that the information read could be stored easily for computational purposes, the computer rapidly became a vital part of the equipment package. Thus the sorter-reader, one of the peripheral elements of the modern data-processing center, was chiefly instrumental in directing bankers' attention to the computer—the central-processing unit.

The high degree of interest in the sorter-reader, in turn, was the natural result of bankers' concern with the mounting problems encountered in their check handling and demand-deposit accounting departments. These two functions presented the greatest opportunity and challenge for cost-cutting for a number of reasons readily traceable to the developments we have been discussing.

Despite the development of proof machines and a variety of bookkeeping machines to replace manual "racking" and posting, check-handling procedures were proving too cumbersome and costly. Because of the limited number of pockets in proof machines (forty pockets in the largest models available) most banks had to handle each check at least twice in its proof-and-transit department. Similarly, the dual-posting system favored by most banks, required that each check be handled twice in the bookkeeping department. As the volume of checks handled grew from year to year, double-handling and sheet-by-sheet posting became luxuries most banks could not afford.

One earlier development in office machines did provide the technical feasibility of single-handling and multiple postings from a single source document—punched-card accounting equipment. These machines were extensively used in many large bank operations, but their applicability to the area under most stress —demand-deposit accounting—was, unfortunately, severely limited. Substantial economies could be achieved if the punched card itself could be used as the check. Most banks, however, believed that customers objected strongly to the size, thickness of stock, and general appearance of a punched-card check.

Many bankers the writer interviewed felt that this common belief was entirely unjustified. These bankers are convinced that the public would have willingly accepted punched-card checks— even in their standard eighty-column size—if they had been suitably introduced and promoted. Many of them believed that, at most, a smaller punched card could have been developed to meet the desires of the most finicky depositors. In support of this argument, it was pointed out that punched-card checks have been widely accepted in corporate agency work (for example, dividend payments), as well as in many corporate payrolls.

Whether justified in their apprehensions or not, the fact remains that comparatively few banks adopted punch-card checks. Several limited them to the lower-status "special account." In 1957 only 14 per cent of the checks handled by American banks were on punch-card stock and of these approximately one half were drawn on the Treasurer of the United States.[5] Thus, the use of punch-card checks by corporate and private depositors accounted for only about 7 per cent of the total volume of checks handled by the banking system in 1957.

If, however, punched-card systems made only a limited *direct* contribution to demand-deposit accounting, their *indirect* contribution was substantial. Punched-card systems familiarized a whole generation of operating officers with many of the fundamental concepts of automatic data processing, its powers and capabilities, and its particular suitability to repetitive, high-volume operations.

Check handling and demand-deposit accounting—besides being troublesome, costly, and high-volume operations—are also subject to tight and demanding deadlines. The need for daily updated records typically requires overnight processing of all demand-deposit items. The threat of drowning in a sea of paper was, therefore, a very real one to many large banks that were already employing a three-shift operation to stem the tide.

For all these reasons, bank operating officers were more than ready to seize on any technological change that promised to provide relief in the hard-pressed areas of check handling and demand-deposit accounting. By the middle 1950's computer technology was beginning to show promise for just such relief. Before proceeding to examine the banking system's first steps towards computer adoption, let us briefly review the spectacular developments in that relatively new field of technology.

2.2. *Electronic Computers Come of Age—The Technological Advances*

Since its first commercial installation, only a decade ago, the electronic computer has been responsible for important break-

---

5. American Bankers Association, Bank Management Commission, *Placement for the Common Machine Language on Checks* (Bank Management Publication 141; April 10, 1957), p. 10.

throughs in three areas of human activity: information processing, problem solving, and automatic control of complex machinery. Whereas our study is primarily concerned with the first two of these areas, it is undoubtedly true that in all its applications the computer represents a major technological advance of real "innovative" proportions, in the Schumpeterian sense of the word. Bright points out that technological advances become significant "when the incremental improvement is an order of magnitude, rather than a percentage of the original figure."[6] In this sense alone, the computer represents a technological change of truly revolutionary proportions. Dr. Richard W. Hamning, director of mathematics research at Bell Telephone Laboratories, observes that most major industrial revolutions were initiated by changes that were merely on the order of ten—an order of magnitude.

The first steam engines were just about 10 times as effective as animal power. Steam locomotives and autos were about 10 times faster than animal drawn vehicles. Aircraft outsped land vehicles by one order of magnitude. Rockets, being more than a magnitude faster than aircraft, quickly replaced them as military weapons. All these single magnitude developments clearly brought profound changes.

Computers, however, bring about a change of six or seven magnitudes. They are up to 10-million times as fast as the mechanical calculators they replace.[7]

A large modern computer can perform three million arithmetic and logical operations a second, and even the smallest of today's machines can perform 150 additions per second. The result is not merely a faster rate of computation or problem solving but, more significantly, the computer makes it practically feasible to tackle and solve problems formerly considered insoluble.

Consider this example, cited by Gregory and Van Horn:

One company . . . that spent three man-months calculating the critical shaft-speed for a steam generator found they could solve the same

6. Bright, "Directions of Technological Change," p. 20.

7. "Special Report: New Tool, New World," *Business Week* (February 29, 1964), p. 75.

problem in forty hours with punched-card machines, in one hour on an early-model electronic computer, in fifteen minutes on a second version, in fifteen seconds on a later version, and in about three seconds on a still newer model. With this last model, the ratio of computer to manual time needed to solve the problem was about 1:500,000.[8]

It is not surprising, therefore, that the literature—both scholarly and popular—is replete with references to the "computer revolution," the "Second Industrial Revolution," the "New Age of the Computer," and so forth.

This revolutionary technological advance sometimes tends to be overlooked in tracing the evolution of data-processing equipment in common business applications. In bank operations, for example, the computer often appears as the successor to punched-card calculating and tabulating equipment. The illusion of rather gradual evolution is heightened by the fact that many computer applications are based on the very same punched-card inputs used in the earlier equipment. Here however the similarity ends. The computer's speed, flexibility, and self-directing ability all represent major technological advances, which in turn are capable of significant advances and changes in the economics of computer use. If there has been little appreciation until recently of the radical nature of computer capability, we must remember that this whole branch of technology is only twenty years old.

It was not until the early 1950's that computer development and experimentation were taken over by the full-time engineering departments of large equipment manufacturers. Further development called for substantial capital investment and a variety of technical, manufacturing, and testing skills and facilities. By 1953 the first UNIVAC-1 was in operation at the Bureau of Census, and by the end of 1954 the first privately used unit was delivered by Remington Rand to the General Electric Company. In late 1955 International Business Machines introduced its Model 650. These two machines became the first commercially

---

8. Robert H. Gregory and Richard L. Van Horn, *Business Data Processing and Programming* (Belmont, California: Wadsworth Publishing Company, Inc., 1963), p. 16.

available computers and mark the beginning of the computer era.

Because of the backgrounds and interests of the early developers, as well as the machine's ability to handle complex computational problems, the computer was initially directed almost exclusively at scientific and mathematical applications. Only in subsequent stages did computer manufacturers begin to adapt their machines for business and commercial use. For the banks, as for most other business organizations, the computer's ability to handle complex mathematical algorithms was of only secondary interest. The chief attractions of the new technology lay in its ability to handle repetitive data at extremely high speeds and to control the operation of peripheral high-speed reading and sorting equipment. As noted earlier, these capabilities held great promise for coping with the growing volume of paper work that threatened to swamp the banking system.

With the installation of UNIVAC and the 650, computer development was off to a fast start. Special-purpose computers were developed, mostly for government use, and a variety of general-purpose models began to appear on the market. It is estimated that in 1964 there were some 14,500 stored-program computers in use throughout the country. In addition there were a few thousand special-purpose military computers, and more than $100,000,000 worth of analog computers used for scientific and engineering work. In the mid-1960's *Business Week* could list at least twenty-four separate companies as major suppliers of digital stored-program computers. Many more manufacturers could be included if specialized military equipment and industrial controls are considered to be computers.

With the advent of the transistor, to replace the vacuum tube, a new order of compactness was introduced, permitting spectacular expansion in computer size. The largest computer at present is Control Data Corporation's 6600 now being completed for the Atomic Energy Commission at a cost of some $7,000,000.

No attempt was made by manufacturers to adapt the computer to bank applications until such adaptation was actively sought by the banking system. Thus the early initiative for the adoption of the new technology by the banks was provided by the users, rather than the suppliers of the equipment. We shall see in the following section how this initiative was provided by the banking system.

2.3. The Banking System's Preparation for Computer Adoption

At approximately the same time that equipment manufacturers were preparing their first standardized computer models, one bank was actively investigating the new technology and attempting to adapt it to its own use. The Bank of America, in cooperation with Stanford Research Institute, began work on its ERMA (Electric Recording Machine Accounting) system. In view of our earlier analysis of the changing conditions in the banking industry, it is rather significant that the first pioneering effort was undertaken by this bank. Almost every one of the change-inducing factors we noted were present in a very marked degree in the Bank of America and its operations.

1. It is the largest bank in the United States—1963 total assets in excess of $12,000,000,000, with 844 branches.

2. Its basic operating philosophy, as laid down by its founder A. P. Giannini, has always been one of "retail" banking; catering to the small depositor, extending bank services to the general public at convenient locations, and vigorously merchandising these services, had long been fundamental management goals.

3. The Bank of America's growth, and hence increase in volume of operations, has been nothing short of spectacular. Even with more than 840 branches in existence it was planning in the mid-1960's to open new ones at the rate of thirty-five to forty per year.

4. The change in its deposit composition underwent the same relative decrease in the ratio of demand deposits to total deposits that was experienced by the rest of the industry, with an even less

favorable shift than the average for the nation. (See Table 2.2.) Bank of America's savings and time deposits increased from almost 50 per cent of total deposits in 1953 to some 54 per cent in 1962. The growing severity of this shift is perhaps most dramatically illustrated by its record in 1962. Out of a rise in total deposits of $620,000,000, only $12,000,000 came in increased demand deposits; the remaining $608,000,000 was represented by a rise in savings and time deposits.

5. California and the West Coast reported the nation's most spectacular growth of savings and loan associations and other financial institutions, aggressively competing with the Bank of America for new customers and depositors.

The second bank active in seeking computer processing was First National City Bank of New York. Although geographically remote from the Bank of America, it showed many similar characteristics in terms of size and banking philosophy, coupled with a long-standing reputation of being the first in any new field. First National City worked closely with International Telephone and Telegraph on the development of both system and equipment for computer processing of its demand-deposit accounting. The fact that neither ERMA nor the ITT system proved to be the type of equipment eventually adopted by the banking system does not detract from the significance of the pioneering work undertaken by both banks. In addition, the pioneer efforts served to focus the banking system's attention on two basically different approaches to mechanized check handling.

In the two banks experimenting with computer processing, the manner in which checks were to be handled physically and read represented a peripheral problem of selecting the most efficient form of input for the new system. For the banking system as a whole, however, the physical handling of checks was a central problem of itself, largely independent of the accounting system with which it would be coupled. Most bankers realized that some mechanization had to be introduced to the check-handling operation, and they soon realized that a single, industry-wide approach was all but imperative.

One of the striking characteristics of the banking system's

2 2

operation is the need for each bank to handle documents initiated by—and drawn on—other banks in the system. Each bank, of necessity, processes checks written on a large number of other banks. It might, in fact, be called upon to handle the checks of any other bank in the country. If *all* checks are to be machine-handled, therefore, a nationwide system must be standardized. Furthermore, if the necessary information is to be machine-readable and if it is to be carried on the check itself, some common language must be developed for the banking system as a whole.

The initiative was taken by the American Bankers Association's Bank Management Commission in early 1954. One of the first problems it studied was whether the machine-readable information was to be carried on the check itself. The issue was clearly posed as a result of the experimentation by the Bank of America and the First National City Bank.

Two basically different approaches had been followed. The Bank of America envisioned a direct-reading system with the necessary information being read off the primary document—the check itself. First National City's system involved reading from a "slave" or "carrier" accompanying each check, on which the needed information had been entered in machine-readable form. This basic difference had to be resolved if the industry was to adopt a single system and if manufacturers were to develop standardized equipment.

On April 5, 1954 the ABA appointed the Technical Subcommittee on Mechanization of Check Handling, consisting of a chairman and five members. The task entrusted to the committee proved to be an extremely complex and demanding one, which took more than five years to complete. It must, however, stand as a monumental achievement in voluntary cooperation.

A detailed account of the many problems tackled and solved by the committee is presented in a series of ABA publications.[9]

---

9. See list of ABA publications in the Bibliography. Also: Robert S. Aldom, *et al., Automation in Banking* (New Brunswick, New Jersey: Rutgers University Press, 1963), Chapter 3.

The writer also gained some insights into the complexity of this task in a lengthy interview with John A. Kley, President of the County Trust Company of White Plains, New York, who acted as chairman of the Technical Committee throughout the project. For purposes of this review it is sufficient to date and highlight only a few of the major steps taken by the committee.

Early in its existence the committee decided in favor of the direct-reading input concept and established as a prerequisite that the check itself be the carrier of the needed information. This decision, together with other minimal specifications for an acceptable system, was published in a pamphlet in 1955 and made available to any manufacturer who might be interested in developing equipment for check processing. The committee then proceeded to test and evaluate several of the then available methods of encoding the desired information on the check. These included two variants of a magnetic-bar code, a fluorescent-ink code visible only under ultraviolet light, and a variety of arabic characters for optical or magnetic scanning. By July 1956 the committee recommended, and the ABA approved, the use of magnetic-ink character recognition (MICR) for all check encoding. An important milestone had been reached, but the task was far from complete.

It was now necessary to select the exact field locations in which the MICR-encoded information was to be placed on the check. At this stage the active cooperation of equipment manufacturers was essential, and in October 1956 the Office Equipment Manufacturers Committee was formed, consisting of representatives of the ten leading companies in the industry. The problem of field location could not be unanimously settled within the Manufacturers Committee, and the decision was referred to the ABA Technical Committee for resolution. In April 1957 the committee decided in favor of MICR encoding along the bottom margin of the check. This settled the general location of coded data, but it was still necessary to specify exact fields and their contents, a process that required the creation of a new code for transit numbers and routing symbols for the entire banking system. In May 1957 another ABA committee was formed to work with the Federal Reserve System with a view to simplifying and standardizing these codes and symbols.

In January 1958 the Technical Committee was able to spell out exact specifications for the coding of information, the items to be encoded, their sequence, and the number of digits to be assigned each field. One major task now remained—the selection of a standard type font that could be read by all manufacturers' equipment. The Type Design Committee was formed in May 1957 as a subcommittee of the Manufacturers Committee. After about a year's work a tentative type font—a modification of the one proposed for Bank of America's ERMA system—was selected. This type design was based on arabic numerals so as to be both man- and machine-readable. In order to insure accuracy and reliability it was decided to subject the new type font to an extensive field-evaluation test. By December 1958 the Technical Committee was convinced of the effectiveness of the type font tested (technically specified E-13B),[10] and recommended its adoption. By April 1959 the committee could issue sufficiently detailed specifications to permit check printers to tool up for the production of the newly approved code. The process of preparing for computerization could now begin in earnest.

Finally, by the end of 1960 the ABA issued its *Check Standards Under the Common Machine Language,* which summarized all detailed specifications developed by its committees over the preceding five years. It described in detail the proper location and placing of that line of odd-looking characters along the bottom edge of checks that has by now become quite familiar to all bank customers. (See Figure 2.2.)

The early pioneers, Bank of America and First National City Bank, abandoned their independent systems despite substantial developmental expenses. IBM and Burroughs Corporation abandoned their own machine-language systems and forgot the cost

---

10. The American Standards Association has recently designated this type font as standard for all MICR-encoded documents. See "ASA Adopts MICR Standards," *Banking* (July 1964), p. 47.

What the Coding on a Check Means

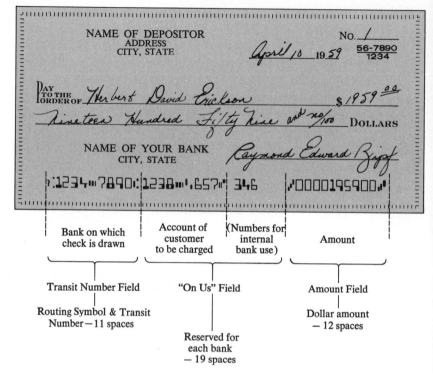

Figure 2.2—Standard Check with MICR Coding and Fields

and time spent in their development. In retrospect these decisions appear obviously justified. At the time they were made, however, they indicate a considerable degree of confidence in the ability of both industries to achieve a standardized language, in its technical feasibility, and in its final adoption by all concerned. It was perhaps most fortunate that the Technical Committee commenced its work at an early enough stage of the process before really substantial development and investment commitments were made by a large number of banks or equipment manufacturers. In 1964 only one bank in the entire United States, the Valley National Bank of Phoenix, Arizona, employed a direct descend-

26

ant of the ITT system originally envisioned for First National City Bank of New York, and this is only used in an internal part of its operations.

Before concluding our review of the accomplishments of the ABA committee we should recall an earlier statement. We stated that, for the banking system as a whole, the computer was carried in on the coattails of its peripheral equipment. This is confirmed by the central issue to which the Technical Committee addressed itself. The development of a common language was primarily an attempt at evolving a method for mechanizing check handling. The most direct result of the committee's work was the development of the high-speed sorter-reader—a device that can read checks at a rate of up to 1,600 a minute and direct them to one of a dozen or more pockets. It must be remembered that in 1954, when the committee started its project, the computer was just making a debut in the commercial field. No one was sure whether it, or some similar device, was going to control and account for the checks processed by the sorter-reader. By a fortunate coincidence the five years that saw the evolution of the common language also saw the rapid development of the computer. By 1958, well before the Technical Committee completed its assignment, it became obvious to all bankers studying the new technology that the coupling of the computer with the sorter-reader presented the ideal combination for both check handling and demand-deposit accounting.

While the Technical Committee was completing its task, the officers of many individual banks seriously considering the adoption of the new technology, engaged in various kinds of preparatory groundwork. Thus by 1960, when full agreement was reached on industry-wide standards, several banks were fully ready to proceed with computer installations. At this point bank automation became both practical and feasible. The new technology had now been formally adopted by the banking system, and, as will be seen in the following section, rapidly began to spread through it.

2 7

2.4. The Rapid Proliferation of Computer Technology

The proliferation of any technological advance through an industry may be viewed, or measured, in two distinct dimensions: first, the "horizontal" diffusion evidenced by a growing number of firms in the industry that utilize the new technology; second, the "vertical" or intensity of exploitation in each individual firm, evidenced by the range and variety of applications to which the new technology is put. Both forms of proliferation are present to a marked degree in bank automation. As this chapter is focused on industry-wide developments, it is best to consider only the horizontal dimension of proliferation here. The vertical dimension is best treated in terms of the range of options open to the individual firm in its exploitation of the new technology. This is done in Chapter IV.

It will be recalled that not until late 1959 or early 1960 did the ABA Technical Committee finally clear all procedural obstacles to the machine-processing of checks. If this event is viewed as the "opening gun" for practical bank automation, then the entire expansion period that can be reviewed (at the time of writing in 1964) is limited to about four and a half years. Considering the brevity of the period, the rate of proliferation of computer installations cannot be described as anything short of spectacular. A period of less than five years—from the introduction of a new technology to its widespread commercial use—appears deceptively short.

Bright identifies at least five major phases in the process of technological innovation:

(a) speculation, suggestion, hypothesis; (b) experimental verification; (c) attempt to apply to useful purpose; (d) commercial introduction; (e) widespread commercial use. . . . This process takes 10 to 15 years usually, to go from phases (b) to (e). If (a) is included, we are often dealing with a 50-year process. There are exceptions, of course, but not as many as some people think.[11]

---

11. Bright, *loc. cit.*

The first two stages deal primarily with the development of computer technology generally. The banking system's adoption of automation is primarily an application of the last three phases. It would be misleading to claim that these three phases were carried out in approximately four years, counting from the 1960 delivery dates of the earliest computer installations. The additional five years of preparation (1955–1960) should properly be added. This additional period actually comes under the third phase—attempt to apply to useful purpose. Bright's estimate of ten to fifteen years for phases (b) to (e) therefore appears applicable to bank automation.

It is the rate of proliferation—the phase of widespread commercial use—that is most impressive. The new technology virtually took the industry by storm, beginning with the largest banks and steadily proceeding to the smaller.

A recent ABA forecast, showing the number and percentage of banks in each size classification with computer installations, emphasizes the rapid and accelerating acceptance of the new technology. By the end of 1963, virtually every bank (92 per cent) with over $500 million in assets could boast a computer installation of its own. Equally impressive is the 85 per cent acceptance by banks between $100 and $500 million and the 52 per cent of banks in the $50 to $100 million category.

In the mid-1960's it was estimated that some 400 banks utilize computers in their operation. Although this is a rather small percentage of the total number of commercial banks in the United States (some 13,500 in all), it is an extremely significant one. The 400 banks involved are all concentrated at the top of the size-distribution, and their relative importance in the banking system becomes clear when we realize that the top 600, or only 4.7 per cent of all commercial banks account for some 69 per cent of total bank deposits.[12] It is as well to bear in mind whenever the figure of 13,500 commercial banks is mentioned that

12. Federal Deposit Insurance Corporation, *Annual Report for 1963* (Washington, D. C.: FDIC, 1964).

almost 10,000, or some 77 per cent, of this total are to be found in the lowest size classifications—those with assets under $10 million. (See Table 2.5.)

Table 2.5—Insured Commercial Banks and Their Deposits Distributed by Bank Size*

Banks with Deposits of	Number of Banks	Total Deposits (in thousands)
Under $1 million	726	$ 540,501
$ 1 to 2 "	2,127	3,166,379
2 to 5 "	4,310	14,285,044
5 to 10 "	2,741	19,176,428
10 to 25 "	1,898	28,867,868
25 to 50 "	575	19,910,352
50 to 100 "	283	19,993,196
100 to 500 "	257	55,163,342
Over $500 "	67	112,010,535
Totals	12,984	273,113,645

* Source: Federal Deposit Insurance Corporation, *Annual Report for December 31, 1963.*

An additional, although indirect, indication of the spread of computer use by banks is provided by the Federal Reserve statement that, as of August 1963, 84.5 per cent of all checks collected through the Federal Reserve banks contained preprinted magnetic-ink coding symbols.

Finally, using its own surveys, the ABA has projected the rate of anticipated computer proliferation through 1975. (See Figure 2.3.) By the end of that period, the ABA expects virtually all banks with over $50 million in assets and a healthy 67 per cent of all banks with assets between $10 and $50 million to be computerized.

It is quite evident then that the new technology has proliferated rapidly throughout the banking system, or at least through that portion of the system that accounts for the bulk of banking operations in the United States.

III

The Individual Bank's
Decision to Automate

In their discussion of business decision making, Newman and Summer identify at least three ways in which a problem—or a need for diagnosis—is identified.[1] The businessman may start with a "felt difficulty," he may sense that "things could be better," or he may compare other firms' accomplishments with those of his own. The existence of these three elements in the bank officers' decision to automate their particular bank is readily borne out by the developments described in the preceding chapter. The several economic and institutional factors noted earlier resulted in markedly "felt difficulties," particularly by the large, retail-oriented banks. The rapid advances in computer technology indicated a technique by which "things could be better." Both these elements were responsible for posing the automation decision to the bank officers considering early adoption of the new technology. Once they decided in favor of automation and the computer proliferation trend described earlier was in full swing, the third element—comparison with other firms' accomplishments—served to sharpen the need for a decision in those banks not already automated.

This chapter will focus on the decision to automate the indi-

---

1. William H. Newman and Charles E. Summer, Jr., *The Process of Management* (Englewood Cliffs, New Jersey: Prentice-Hall, Inc., 1961), p. 263.

vidual bank and the relevance of the economic and technological factors considered prior to this decision. While, obviously, there can be many individual differences in the decision-making process in each bank, there are sufficiently broad similarities to be able to present a composite picture.

3.1. Typical Steps in the Decision to Automate

The "felt difficulty" and the opportunity to "make things better" are usually formalized and evaluated in a so-called feasibility study. This study is a commonly used approach in the consideration of any electronic data-processing proposal. The scope and content of feasibility studies have been described in some detail in the literature. A good example of this treatment may be found in Gregory and Van Horn.[2] For this reason only a brief outline of a typical bank automation-feasibility study will be presented here.

The practice in most banks has been to assign a senior operating officer or an automation committee the task of investigating computer feasibility and recommending action to top management. A study team or task force is often formed to assemble the necessary data, consider new systems and procedures, and provide liaison with a variety of outside experts. Equipment manufacturers and/or management consultants are called upon in almost every single case.

Regardless of the sources of expertise, a sound feasibility study should cover the following major steps.

1. A thorough survey is made of current operating procedures, volume statistics, policies, personnel utilization, and relevant costs.

2. Robert Gregory and Richard Van Horn, *Automatic Data-Processing Systems* (Belmont, California: Wadsworth Publishing Company, Inc., 1963), Chapter 16.

2. New systems are developed in rough form only, in no more detail than is needed to determine overall equipment requirements and approximate processing times.

3. Utilizing the second step, broad equipment specifications are determined and all one-time costs are computed.

4. The economic feasibility of the new system is evaluated on the basis of the first three steps. "Before" and "after" costs are computed, and potential savings are projected. It is desirable to be extremely conservative in this phase of the study.

5. Other-than-tangible cost factors, both pro and con, should be presented. Both tangible and intangible benefits should be considered, not only for the immediate future, but for several years ahead. Often a period up to as long as ten years is considered, using the best available forecasts and estimates of future operational requirements.

6. Finally a step-by-step program and timetable is presented for the full implementation of the new system.

Once the feasibility study is completed (and assuming it recommends adoption of electronic data-processing systems) the phase of detailed system design and equipment selection begins. Detailed flow sheets show the specific demands each bank's system will place on the equipment to be used. These are translated to equipment specifications and, typically, several manufacturers are asked to submit proposals. The equipment proposals must then be evaluated. This is often a complex technical task, as different equipment configurations will usually present a variety of advantages and disadvantages that may not be directly comparable. For this reason bank managements often rely on outside consultants to select the equipment for them. The use of an outsider also tends to neutralize some of the biases of employees familiar with a particular manufacturer's equipment or of other financial or service ties with a particular manufacturer. Nevertheless, equipment selection is still, to some extent, subjective. Not only must the technical specifications of each proposal be weighed, but also less tangible elements such as the manufacturer's experience with similar installations, the caliber of his

3 3

service and maintenance, his willingness to accept trade-ins on discarded equipment, the locally available back-up facilities for the contemplated equipment, and the availability and quality of "software." Where the new system must tie in with other machines already on hand, their compatability must also be considered. Finally, it is necessary to evaluate the costs and difficulties which may be involved in any future attempt to expand the equipment's capacity or sophistication. All too often the configuration showing best immediate results may prove a poor second or also-ran when projections for the next five years are considered.

Once this phase is completed, a detailed implementation program is developed. It must provide for the execution of the many details before conversion. Forms, checks, and reports must be redesigned, computer programs must be written, technicians and operators must be trained or hired, the site must be prepared, and a detailed conversion program set up. In addition to technical preparations it is necessary to prepare both bank employees and customers for the conversion to electronic data-processing (EDP). Detailed discussion of this preparation is beyond the scope of this study. Suffice it to state that securing the active cooperation of both employees and customers is an essential prerequisite to successful bank automation.

Finally the bank is ready for the conversion. Usually, a pilot system is tested on a limited number of accounts to get as much "debugging" completed before full operations are begun. At the same time all necessary records must be converted to tape, card, or other media of operation. In almost every case it has been desirable to run a parallel operation of the old system for a short time after conversion. In the event of a serious malfunction or unanticipated difficulties, disruption of bank operations is avoided by reference to the conventional system's records and reports.

It is quite evident that the procedure outlined here is a rather lengthy one. The experience of Booz, Allen & Hamilton indicates that the following realistic time allowances should be anticipated: feasibility study—three months; systems design and equipment

34

selection—six months; implementation program—fourteen to eighteen months; and conversion—six to twelve months. The entire process may run to two and a half or three years. It is also a costly one. As we shall see in subsequent sections of this chapter, one-time implementation costs can be as high as $1½ million for a large bank.

The long delay between conception and implementation of automation, as noted, has discouraged the plunge into computer processing without extensive soul-searching. Relatively few computers have been adopted merely to "keep up with the Joneses" or the Banks of America. A review of the responses to the ABA survey indicate that where there have been disappointments they have been primarily traceable to technical errors in systems planning or to lack of active follow-up by top management. Most decisions to automate banks were made with at least a conscientious attempt at a rational, economic evaluation of the alternatives.

1402198

3.2. Economic and Technical Focus of the Decision to Automate

Automation feasibility studies, as their name implies, basically consider two problems. First, the technical question—can it be done? Second, the economic question—is it worth doing? Whereas the technical feasibility of bank automation posed a serious problem to the early pioneers in the new technology, later converts paid progressively less attention to it. The degree of risk and uncertainty as to *technical* feasibility was drastically and rapidly reduced, as will be seen in subsequent sections of this chapter. For most banks considering automation during the first half of the 1960's the *economic* evaluation was of paramount importance. Let us, therefore, consider this element first before we return to further discussion of the technical factors in the feasibility study.

The economic considerations in any automation decision basically consist of balancing costs against returns. "Returns" may be monetary or nonmonetary, tangible or intangible. In the case of bank automation, "returns" were primarily viewed as savings in operating costs—either immediate or long run. Our review of economic and institutional pressures on the banking system readily explains the reasons for the banker's early interest in the computer as a cost-saving device.

Although expressed in a number of different ways in many interviews with bank officers, the underlying attraction of the computer was its promise to cope with growing volumes of paperwork without corresponding increases in clerical staffs. Some officers talked in terms of immediate reductions in clerical costs, others in terms of maintaining present staffs to meet the growing volume demands of the future. Some focused on the cost of clerical work, others on the difficulty and inefficiency of expanding clerical departments, or the shortages of qualified personnel, or rising turnover rates, or inadequate supervision.

In the ABA's recent National Automation Survey, out of 697 banks responding to the query "reasons for our decision to automate," 570 indicated that freezing or reducing operating costs was a major factor, another 111 considered it a minor factor and only 16 considered it no factor. Other factors mentioned and the relative weight assigned to éach are shown in Table 3.1. It should be noted that the stated reasons "improve internal systems," "meet competition," and "improve management reports" may all contain a cost-saving dimension, depending upon the respondent's interpretation of the exact meaning.

It is equally significant that all the feasibility studies examined by the writer placed their main emphasis on the economics of the proposed conversion. In every case the "returns" against which the cost of the installation was compared consisted almost exclusively of savings in operating costs. If the economic evaluation of cost versus savings was not the *sole* consideration in the automation decision, it was certainly a major component.

Table 3.1—"Reasons for Our Decision to Automate"—Survey Responses of 697 Banks*

REASON	Frequency of Citing As a—					
	MAJOR FACTOR		MINOR FACTOR		NO FACTOR	
	No.	Per cent	No.	Per cent	No.	Per cent
Freeze or reduce operating costs	570	82	111	16	16	2
Improve internal systems	494	71	171	24	19	3
Increase flexibility for new business	262	38	284	41	90	13
Meet competition	235	34	250	36	155	22
Enable bank to offer new services	278	40	265	38	98	14
Tighten audit and control	251	36	313	45	72	10
Improve management reports	302	43	279	40	55	8
Other	58	8	4	—	0	—

*Source: ABA, National Automation Survey (1963).

Another common characteristic evident in bank-automation proposals concerned technical considerations mentioned earlier. An important element of the proposal to automate is the basic approach taken toward the redesign of existing systems and procedures. Such systems design can be tackled on any one of several levels. Gregory and Van Horn identify four levels, which "range from merely simplifying the present system, through mechanization, to developing either a new data system or a completely new management information system."[3] Each approach depends on the degree of freedom open to the designer and the extent to which inputs, data flows, files and outputs are considered essentially fixed.

Bank-automation studies typically treat all these elements largely as givens. The result is that initial computer applications generally fall in the "mechanization" category, as far as check-handling is concerned, and in a rather elementary "data system" category, as far as bookkeeping is concerned. The introduction of the computer, therefore, creates only relatively minor changes in information content or its flow. Its most significant result is the substitution of high-speed equipment for manual clerical work or slower-speed calculating machines. This almost exclusive view of

---

3. Gregory and Van Horn, *Business Data Processing and Programming*, pp. 136–144.

the computer as a production machine—a fast pair of hands guided by a low-level brain—can be traced back to the banking system's earliest interest in the new technology. In its progress report of 1956, the ABA's Bank Management Commission described its task as a search for a "replacement for the hands, eyes, and the more automatic phases of mental activity."[4]

The decision to automate, therefore, was perceived in economic terms that stressed cost-saving considerations and a technical frame of reference that viewed the computer as a high-output paperwork processing machine. This inevitably served to direct bank managements' attention to one particular area of operations, namely, check-handling.

The ABA survey previously cited indicates that of 348 responding banks which at that time operated computer installations 82.2 per cent already employed the computer in demand-deposit accounting for regular checking accounts and 79.5 per cent used it for special checking accounts. Only 46 per cent of these banks utilized computer processing for savings-deposit accounting and less than 25 per cent for corporate trust work. Responses to the question "internal applications status" are shown in Table 3.2.

Table 3.2—"Internal Applications Status" in Deposit and Loan Accounting—Survey Responses of 348 Banks*

APPLICATION	BANKS EMPLOYING IT	
	Number	Per cent
Deposits		
Special Checking	287	82.2
Regular Checking	276	79.5
Savings	161	46.0
Proof and Transit	87	24.9
Loans		
Consumer	135	38.6
Mortgage	74	21.2
Commercial	36	8.8

* Source: ABA, National Automation Survey (1963).

4. American Bankers Association, Bank Management Commission, *A Progress Report—Mechanization of Check Handling* (Bank Management Publication 140; 1956), p. 4.

Perhaps even more significant, in terms of the decision to automate, is the response from banks who were making plans for computer adoption at the time of the ABA survey. The relevant query to them was worded: "After we automate, our plans will include the following:". (See Table 3.3.) Out of 419 banks re-

Table 3.3—Applications to Be Installed by Banks Planning Automation—Survey Responses of 419 Banks to: "After We Automate Our Plans Will Include:"*

APPLICATION	BANKS PLANNING TO INSTALL IT	
	Number	Per cent
Demand Deposits	408	97.6
Savings	278	66.3
Installment Loans	245	58.2
Proof and Transit	206	49.2
Other Loans	114	27.2
Personal Trust	60	14.3
Other	51	12.2

* Source: ABA, National Automation Survey (1963).

sponding, 408 banks (97.6 per cent) checked demand-deposit accounting. In the same vein, of the forty banks for which detailed cost data was provided by Booz, Allen & Hamilton—a sample that includes twenty banks that operate their own computer installations and twenty banks that have formed cooperative data-processing centers—we find that all forty banks rely on the computer for demand-deposit accounting. Of these forty banks, sixteen utilize this application exclusively, while the remaining twenty-four couple it with one or more of the following: fourteen banks, with proof and transit; nine, with installment loans; seven, with personal trust; three, with corporate trust; and one, with other applications. (See Table 3.4.)

Check-handling and demand-deposit accounting thus appeared almost universally as the first bank operations to be automated. They, in fact, provided the major economic incentive for adopting the new technology even in cases where additional benefits were anticipated from the conversion. The following

Table 3.4—Initial Computer Applications in 40 Commercial Banks*

	Initial Applications Installed			
	IN 20 BANKS WHICH OPERATE OWN COMPUTER INSTALLATION		IN 20 BANKS WHICH OPERATE COOPERATIVE CENTER	
Application	Number	Per cent	Number	Per cent
Demand Deposits	20	100	20	100
Proof and Transit	4	20	10	50
Installment Loans	9	45	—	—
Personal Trust	7	35	—	—
Corporate Trust	3	15	—	—
Other	1	5	—	—

* Source: Booz, Allen & Hamilton, Inc., Feasibility Studies.

section examines these incentives in quantitative terms—cost and return considerations for a wide variety of commercial banks.

3.3. The Economics of Bank Automation—Costs Versus Savings

If bank operating officers were eagerly casting about for some means of reducing clerical and handling costs; let us examine the extent to which computer processing could promise to deliver such savings. To date there has been no published data to indicate specific costs or savings resulting from bank automation. With the kind cooperation of Booz, Allen & Hamilton, the author was able to analyze summarized cost data for forty of their client banks. For obvious reasons the identities of the banks involved were not disclosed, nor was any other information that might violate the confidential client-consultant relationship. As a further measure of identity-protection, the individual bank data which we analyzed and correlated will not be presented here. Only summaries of ranges and medians for a group of banks will be tabulated.

A number of comments about this newly available data are pertinent before we proceed to an analysis of them. The figures analyzed were taken from feasibility studies, which the consultant conducted for each client bank. The studies are based on a detailed survey of existing costs and conditions, projected costs and savings upon completing the computer installation, as well as a longer-term projection of operating costs with and without the computer. The relevant current costs are computed only for those functions and operations that will be affected by the conversion to the new system. These are frequently difficult to isolate and quantify. Some of the affected tasks represent only one part of a bundle of activities performed by an individual, the remainder of the bundle being unaffected by the proposed conversion. In such cases it is necessary to separate out the man-hours involved, often in several geographically separated departments, branches, or offices. Similarly, the current costs of any machinery and equipment in use must be allocated so as to separate out those elements of the cost that would be affected by conversion to computer processing.

The feasibility study's post-conversion costs, it must be clearly understood, are *projections,* not actual record costs after the installation. They are developed by careful computations based on systems analysis, run timing, down-time allowances, and considerable past experience in similar applications. Despite every attempt at conservatism, projections unfortunately do not have the same authoritative ring as actual measured costs, which— equally unfortunately—are costly to obtain and hence are generally not available. For purposes of our analysis, however, it may be argued that the projected costs are the more meaningful. In the first place, these figures are presented to management *before* computer installation is undertaken; hence they form the basis on which management makes the decision as to the desirability of the installation. These figures are the projected savings potential that management must take into account in weighing the benefits of automation against its costs, which are also, to some extent, projected. It may also be pointed out that computed costs are closer to the true or "rational" costs of computer operation than any actual figures that may be obtained within a year or so of installation. The latter would be subject to distortion due to the no-layoff policy commonly adopted by most banks, the nonrepresentative costs of the shakedown period of the new system, and the extremely difficult-to-isolate costs of new subfunctions or by-product information that were not previously available. Finally periodic follow-up visits to client banks indicate that management believes that the projected costs and savings presented in the feasibility study have, by and large, proved reasonably accurate in subsequent operations.

In all fairness to the banking system, it should be pointed out here that the same difficulties in obtaining cost data for automation studies are common in all industrial firms. Bright notes four reasons to explain this dearth of valid data:

1. Some firms that were willing to cooperate in every other way felt that cost and labor figures . . . were too competitive or otherwise confidential to be released. . . .
2. In a surprising number of cases the data did not exist. . . .
3. Often the data were not usable because so many extraneous factors influenced the figures. How can the savings . . . be determined when the cost center was simultaneously expanded, several departments consolidated, a new product introduced, and new overhead items included . . . during the automation program?
4. Many data were not comparable in a "before automation" and "after automation" sense. . . .[5]

In many interviews with bank officers, the writer was rather surprised by the frequent admission that banks generally maintain far less comprehensive and accurate cost records than do their industrial clients. Not only are internal cost allocations less refined but there is also far less interbank uniformity in accounting practices and treatment. It must be recalled that there are no prescribed standard conventions for bank reporting comparable to the SEC or New York Stock Exchange codes for publicly traded corporations.

Before proceeding with an analysis of the Booz, Allen & Hamilton data, a further word of explanation is necessary in connection with their practice for projecting longer-term savings. A

---

5. Bright, *Automation and Management,* pp. 9–10.

typical feasibility study includes a comparison of projected operating costs—with and without the computer—for several years beyond the proposed installation date. A period of seven to ten years is often used. Costs are computed by extrapolating from present figures at assumed rates of annual increases in (1) volume of activity, and (2) clerical wage rates. These are usually found to range between 2 per cent and 4 per cent in most bank studies. In some instances the projected increases in volume of transactions indicate the need for future additions to the equipment. Such additional equipment is, therefore, programmed within the forecast period, and its costs and savings are included in the computation of long-run benefits.

For each year's computation, savings are calculated *net* of equipment rental and maintenance. Nonrecurring costs chargeable to the conversion are *not* included in operating costs but are treated as "implementation costs."

The data we analyzed for the forty-bank sample is condensed and summarized in Tables 3.5 and 3.6, for banks with individually and cooperatively owned computer installations respectively. The following facts emerge from an analysis of the data summarized in Table 3.5.

1. Reductions in personnel (number of employees involved in the automated operations) are achievable by all banks for which this data was available. Such reductions range from 8 to 336 employees, with 66 as a median, 30 and 166 as the first and third quartile, respectively. As a percentage of the existing number of employees in the affected operations, personnel reductions range from 10 per cent to 67 per cent, averaging approximately 42 per cent. It is significant that a fairly substantial 32 per cent reduction in number of employees is indicated even in the case of one bank that shows *negative* savings for the first year of computer operation. This means that machine rental and other non-payroll expenses exceeded the salaries and wages of the displaced employees.

The reduction in the numbers of personnel was found to be closely correlated with the size of the bank (coefficient of correla-

Table 3.5—Summarized Data for 20 Banks, from Feasibility Studies by Booz, Allen & Hamilton, Inc.

	RANGE		MEDIAN
	Low	High	
Bank size, by deposits (in millions of $)	18	3,551	370
Number of checking accounts (in thousands)	10	550*	60*
Activity, by average daily transactions (in thousands)	10	450*	61*
Implementation costs (in thousands of $)	51	1,608	340
Payback period (in years)	1½	8	2½
Number of personnel in affected departments			
Before automation	12	741	182
After automation	4	508	94
Reduction due to automation			
Number	8	336	66
Per cent	10	67	48
Projected operating costs, first year of automation (in thousands of $)			
If not automated	77	5,294	884
With automation	75	5,144	777
Estimated savings	(217)	1,304	95
Projected operating costs, fifth year of automation (in thousands of $)			
If not automated	99	6,443	1,031
With automation	80	4,716	877
Estimated savings	19	1,727	156
Projected operating costs, eighth year of automation† (in thousands of $)			
If not automated	666	7,845	1,342
With automation	524	5,658	1,077
Estimated savings	137	2,187	203

* Estimated; these figures were not available for largest bank in sample.
† For 12 banks only; not available for other 8.

tion $r = .783$), and even more closely correlated with the volume of activity as measured by the average daily number of transactions ($r = .961$).

2. Savings in operating costs were projected in the first year after installation for all but four of the banks analyzed. Of these, only one bank shows a significant loss ($217,000), whereas two others indicate a nominal loss of $1,000, and a third a loss of $8,000. First-year savings, as a percentage of relevant pre-automation costs, range from −4.4 per cent to +24.6 per cent, averaging +10.7 per cent.

Cost savings in the first year of operation, like personnel reductions, show a close correlation with volume of activity,

44

Table 3.6—Summarized Data for 19 Banks Operating Cooperative Centers, from Feasibility Studies by Booz, Allen & Hamilton, Inc.

	RANGE		MEDIAN
	Low	High	
Bank size, by deposits (in millions of $)	5	100	22
Implementation costs (in thousands of $)	4	61	13
Number of personnel in affected departments*			
Before automation	6	27	18
After automation	2	11	7
Reduction due to automation			
Number	4	19	7
Per cent	39	76	61
Projected operating costs, first year of automation (in thousands of $)			
If not automated	22	153	45
With automation	11	132	39
Estimated Savings	(1)	33	8
Projected operating costs, fifth year of automation (in thousands of $)			
If not automated	27	180	60
With automation	16	148	41
Estimated savings	1	51	11
Projected operating costs, eighth year of automation (in thousands of $)†			
If not automated	35	201	57
With automation	33	159	49
Estimated savings	2	41	12

* For 10 banks only; not available for other 9.
† For 9 banks only; not available for other 10.

($r = .831$), and only a limited correlation ($r = .591$) with bank size.

3. It is interesting to note the substantially greater savings indicated for the fifth year after installation, as compared with the first. For the nineteen banks for which this data is available, total fifth-year savings are more than double those indicated for the first year—actually a rise of 112 per cent. These projections point up the fact that in most bank conversions the computer configuration selected provides a capacity well in excess of immediate needs. Thus, as volume of activity continues to grow, comparatively minor additions of personnel and equipment can adequately absorb this growth.

4. "Implementation costs," as defined in feasibility studies, and summarized in Tables 3.5 and 3.6, refer to all one-time costs

associated with the evaluation, preparation, and conversion to automation. Typically they include such items as planning and programming, consulting services, site preparation, purchase of any equipment or fixtures, costs of record conversion, employee training, and parallel operation during the conversion period.

It can be seen that implementation costs are often quite substantial. In two of the larger banks they were close to $1½ million. The decision to convert to computer processing obviously could not be taken lightly or without the direct approval of top management for this reason alone—quite aside from many other ramifications in respect to bank operations and customer relations.

5. From a bank management's point of view, perhaps the most important factor in evaluating the savings potential of a proposed computer installation is the anticipated payback period—that is, the number of years of cumulative cost savings required to pay back the initial implementation cost. This is an indication of the effectiveness of the investment in the new technology.

In the banks studied, payback periods ranged from one and a half to eight years, with a 3.3-year average and a two-and-a-half-year median.

The data summarized in Tables 3.5 and 3.6 serve to confirm, with actual case experience, the statements often heard but rarely documented that computer installations do indeed "pay for themselves." It has already been pointed out that it is extremely difficult to compute actual costs and savings directly attributable to automation. Most bank officers who, when interviewed by the writer, would hazard a guess, estimated the payback period to be between two and three years. All admitted this represented a rough estimate at best.

In terms of the decision to automate, therefore, it is evident that economic considerations also present a persuasive argument for adopting the new technology. In the large majority of cases the potential savings in operating costs represent an extremely attractive return on the investment in implementation costs. The correlations noted further indicate that this return increases with the size of the bank and even more so with the degree of its "retail" orientation. These conclusions confirm the explanation advanced earlier for the innovating role assumed by the Bank of America and First National City Bank of New York. They also explain why proliferation of computer installation began with the largest banks in the system and progressed down the size scale.

3.4. Aids to Proliferation—A Comparative Case Study: Pioneer Versus New Recruit

A brief recounting of the highlights of the experiences of two banks in deciding upon and implementing a computer installation will illustrate the changing nature of this process as bank automation gains acceptance and popularity.

FIDELITY BANK AND TRUST COMPANY[6]—A PIONEER IN AUTOMATION

Fidelity, one of the largest banks in the country, is in the over-one-billion-dollar deposit classification. As far back as the early 1940's this bank had a methods research department with considerable experience in punched-card systems and a keen interest in innovation. By 1954 this department had perceived the electronic computer as a likely new aid to bank operations. Its officers began to study several experimental system designs even before suitable computers were available commercially. When the IBM 650 was announced, the bank's personnel suggested a number of modifications and promptly rented the machine for experimentation. It is interesting to note that, although they realized that this particular piece of equipment was most unlikely to be used in actual operations, they needed it as an instructional tool. As the officer in charge explained the situation to the writer, here was the beginning of a new technology that was bound to affect bank operations. No one was sure where or how such effects would be felt, but it was agreed that the new technology

---

6. Fictitious name.

had to be investigated—and at first hand. Top management was persuaded to approve a budget for research and study purposes, without a specific application in mind.

In early 1958 an IBM 650 was installed, and its capabilities were closely investigated. Demand-deposit accounting was one of the earliest applications attempted. The technical feasibility and reliability of several accounting systems was painstakingly tested until a single system was evolved. In order to try it out, all bank-employee accounts were converted to computer processing. These accounts—a "captive audience" in effect—were used to debug the original system and improve its programming. The entire operation was run by the personnel of the methods research department. When convinced of the feasibility and advantages of the new system, the bank placed orders for the latest computer available then, the IBM 7070.

In September 1961 the new equipment was installed and all checking accounts were gradually converted. The conversion was implemented on a branch-by-branch plan. The entire demand-deposit conversion (involving over 150,000 accounts) was completed in just over two years. In the early conversion stages, parallel operation of both old and new systems was considered essential, but this was soon abandoned. The system's developers were convinced that the final computer program, representing some six months' careful work, contained sufficient audit and control features to insure complete accuracy and reliability. By the end of 1963 all checking accounts except for some deliberate exceptions were converted to computer processing.

During the five years from the first experimentation with demand-deposit accounting until complete conversion of all checking accounts, the methods research department was not exclusively tied up with this application. Fidelity Bank developed an approach that permitted this department to continue its concentration on research while turning completed projects over to operating departments. As each application successfully completed its trial runs in the methods research department it was "spun off," together with a few of the key personnel responsible

4 8

for its development, to the appropriate operating department for its day-to-day operations. Methods research was thus relieved of operating responsibility and could proceed with advanced development work on other applications. The continuous loss of personnel and the need for their replacement was clearly recognized as a disadvantage of this approach. However the bank officers felt that several sizable advantages far outweighed this difficulty: a trained staff went along with each application to assure its success in operation and, in time, a nucleus of qualified technicians was dispersed throughout the several banking departments. These technicians were all trained by the methods research department, were closely familiar with its objectives and methodology, and proved to be excellent links for future communication and liaison. Methods research could, therefore, continue acting as an inside consultant when unforeseen problems or the need for systems modification arose in any bank operation.

At the time of writing in 1964 the methods research department employed some forty people with a wide variety of backgrounds and skills. Use of outside consultants was restricted to periodic reviews or audits of the department's internally developed programs and ideas. Although computer applications received the major attention of the department, they were by no means its sole concern. A variety of other methods and ideas had been studied and developed by the same department. It should also be pointed out here that most bankers and technical experts interviewed by the writer generally agreed that Fidelity Bank and Trust, with its methods research department, was one of the prominent leaders in the banking system's movement to automation.

MERCHANTS MIDWEST BANK[7]—A MORE RECENT CONVERT

This bank represents a striking contrast with Fidelity Bank and Trust in size, location, and operations. Merchants showed 1963 total assets in the $100–$250 million class. It is located in a large

---

7. Fictitious name.

midwest city, where it has twenty-six branches in the city and surrounding communities. The accounting and servicing of demand deposits, however, are almost identical in operation in the two banks. It is interesting therefore to examine the conversion experienced by Merchants and, subsequently, contrast the two experiences.

In early 1960, Merchants first became interested in the possibility of automating its demand-deposit and installment-loan operations. By December 1960 a feasibility study was authorized by top management, and one operating officer was assigned the task. It took approximately one year to complete the study and select the equipment to be ordered. The study and recommendations were approved by the bank's operations committee (consisting of eight officers) in December 1961. At this point two assistants were assigned to the officer in charge for the purpose of programming and planning for conversion.

In February 1962 an IBM 1401 was ordered, and by November of that year all hardware was installed and ready to run. No trial runs were attempted on this equipment. "Debugging" was done on the premises of a neighboring bank with 1401's already in operation. It took some forty-five days to convert all special-checking accounts to tape records and only two days of parallel operations to prove out the new system. Some 35,000 installment-loan accounts were converted over one weekend and were placed in full operation without any parallel running. No major troubles were experienced in any of the conversions. Some minor problems were encountered, but these were readily detected and eliminated.

The time and cost of computer programming were drastically cut by reliance on IBM's prepackaged program. Only three days' work was involved in modifying this standard program to the bank's own needs. Bank officers estimated a saving of approximately $25,000 in programming costs, as a result of using the packaged program.

No outside consultants were employed throughout this program. Three equipment manufacturers were asked to submit proposals based on the bank's own specifications and job descriptions. The manufacturer's claims for their equipment were verified against the experience of other banks using such equipment. No outside experts or technicians were hired by the bank for the planning, implementation, or routine operation of the new system. All the necessary training in EDP, computers, and so forth, was provided by the local IBM office. The bank reports that no changes in organizational structure were made before, during, or after conversion.

In 1964, Merchants' computer installation was handling approximately 50,000 checking accounts, 39,000 installment loans, 17,000 Christmas Club accounts, 9,000 mortgages, and some miscellaneous accounting applications. When first installed, the payback period for the new system was estimated at about four years. A sizable increase in checking accounts since that time was believed to have reduced this early estimate. In summary, the bank views its conversion to computer operations as orderly, successful, and free of any major difficulty or disruption.

SIGNIFICANT DIFFERENCES IN THE TWO EXPERIENCES

A number of specific differences are clearly evident in the automation experience of the two banks just described. Perhaps the most striking difference, however, is to be found in the more abstract terms of the risk and uncertainty inherent in the decision-making process. In contrast to Fidelity's painstaking experimentation, Merchants approached automation with complete confidence in the technical feasibility and reliability of the new technology. Little or no time had to be spent in proving the computer's ability to handle the tasks to be assigned it. The experience of some two hundred banks was proof of the practicability of the new technology. Its basic adaptability to bank operations was no longer in doubt. All that remained was to determine how Merchants' individual installation would be best executed. Even this task was approached with extreme confidence and a minimum diversion of resources. In short, the entire conversion was treated more in the nature of a routine operational process than a research or development project.

In addition to general attitude and approach, a number of concrete differences can be seen in the two experiences. These differences reflect important advances in the technology in the intervening years. They vividly illustrate some of the major factors responsible for the rapid and accelerating rate of proliferation already noted.

1. The time and professional-skill levels required for feasibility studies had decreased markedly, and with them the costs of investigating the new technology. Under these conditions, however, a relatively low level of systems design is almost inevitable. Bank officers with limited experience, resources, and time are not likely to develop what Gregory and Van Horn describe as "management information systems." A more probable result would be the design of "mechanization-level" systems, or the initiation of systems designed by others. It should be noted, however, that even under the accelerated schedule it was a full year before equipment was selected.

2. A substantially broader range of equipment had become available for selection. At least six manufacturers were active in the field when Merchants decided to automate (although only three were asked to submit bids). Each manufacturer, in addition, could recommend equipment in a wide range of sizes, speeds, and configurations. Significantly, smaller-capacity computers at lower rental costs were now available. The smaller user could more conveniently tailor his equipment rental to his needs. Equally important, most of the available equipment had been proved out in actual use in many similar bank operations.

3. The widespread publicity given bank automation, in both the popular and trade press, had served to familiarize bankers with its advantages and profitability. This was coupled with greatly intensified sales and promotion efforts by the manufacturers. As each equipment manufacturer introduced new computers to its line, advertising and sales campaigns mounted rapidly. The keen competition between computer manufacturers

was a significant factor in the proliferation of bank automation.[8]

4. A wide body of experience had developed within the banking system, and a great degree of cooperation between banks had permitted exchange of this experience. Merchants had learned much from other banks' experience and even used others' equipment for its own trials.

5. The availability of prepackaged programs from equipment manufacturers had substantially reduced the skill levels and costs involved in systems designs and detail programming. Such prepackaging is made possible by the uniform requirements of check processing in all banks and is a direct dividend of the common language adopted by the bank system. (Further discussion of the manufacturers' contribution is presented in Chapter V.)

6. With standardization of practices and the growing availability of manufacturers' training programs, it was possible for Merchants to train its own personnel in the new technology without hiring trained outsiders. Such training, in sufficient depth to achieve a successful conversion, was accomplished on a part-time basis and in a relatively short time. Between manufacturers' training programs and the willingly shared experience of other banks, operating officers evidently can be qualified to act as their own technicians. The limitation, in terms of creativity in systems design, has already been pointed out.

In a period of four or five years then the acceptance and understanding of the new technology rises remarkably. The aura of mystery surrounding EDP and computers is largely dispelled and is replaced by total confidence in their capability. The road to automation for the new recruit is simpler, easier, and less costly. This phenomenon, described as "leapfrogging" in some of the current technical literature, is not new to economic theory. We can note how aptly Joseph Schumpeter's description fits the situation, substituting "banks" or "firms" for "people":

---

8. Cf. Gilbert Burck, "The Assault on Fortress IBM," *Fortune,* Vol. LXIX, No. 6 (June 1964), p. 112.

. . . the carrying out of new combinations is difficult and only accessible to people with certain qualities. . . . However, if one or a few have advanced with success many of the difficulties disappear. Others can then follow these pioneers, as they will clearly do under the stimulus of the success now attainable. Their success again makes it easier, through the increasingly complete removal of the obstacles . . . for more people to follow suit, until finally the innovation becomes familiar and the acceptance of it a matter of free choice.[9]

The same tendency is discussed by Veblen in *Imperial Germany and the Industrial Revolution.* Two apt abstracts from this work are included in *The Portable Veblen* under the headings "On the Merits of Borrowing" and "On the Penalty of Taking the Lead."[10]

It remains to be seen whether the elimination of some of the built-in delay and high cost of automation noted earlier will lead to improperly conceived or poorly designed computer installations. Whether or not banks will embark on automation simply because it is the fashionable trend, with little or no regard for the economic and technical limitations applicable to their individual operations, is also yet to be seen.

3.5. Some Obstacles to Proliferation of Bank Automation

ECONOMIC OBSTACLES

The quantitative analysis of cost and return, presented earlier in this chapter, clearly points out a major economic obstacle. "Return," in the form of potential savings through automation, was found to be closely correlated with bank size and activity. Banks below a given size find automation uneconomical in terms of the savings generated. With existing equipment and tech-

9. Joseph A. Schumpeter, *The Theory of Economic Development* (Galaxy Edition; New York: Oxford University Press, 1961), p. 228.
10. Max Lerner (ed.), *The Portable Veblen* (New York: The Viking Press, 1961), pp. 349 and 365.

niques, a rough rule-of-thumb places this minimal size at around $5 million in deposits and/or 20,000 checking accounts. Some 13,000 banks, or approximately 96 per cent of all commercial banks in the United States, fall below these figures. Their contribution to total banking activity, however, accounts for a mere 30 per cent. Nevertheless, they are subject to the same economic and institutional pressures as the larger banks. In some respects, in fact, competitive pressures may prove more critical for the smaller banks. It is not surprising, therefore, to find the alert small bank discovering effective responses to the seeming impasse of acute need and and insufficient size. Four solutions had been developed by the mid-1960's to meet the small bank's automation problem.

1. The cooperative data-processing center. A group of small banks jointly own and operate a computer installation. Successful examples of this arrangement are the Bank Computer Center of Connecticut (nine participating members) and the Bay State Computer Center of Waltham, Massachusetts (six member banks). In addition to the Federal Bank Service Corporation Act of October 23, 1962, in some states special enabling legislation was needed to make such inter-bank ventures permissible.

2. Service by correspondent bank. Under this arrangement small banks obtain computer services from their larger city correspondents. The small bank may contract to buy only those services that it finds economical or advantageous. The servicing bank charges a fee, which usually consists of a fixed charge per account serviced plus a variable charge per transaction.

3. Use of a commercial service bureau. In most metropolitan areas there are commercially operated service bureaus supplying computer processing for any business user in their area. These are usually privately owned or may be run and operated by one of the major equipment manufacturers. Banks may contract for any type of service they desire.

4. Joint ventures with nonbanking firms. In some instances banks have found it feasible to share a computer installation with a nonbanking neighbor. Costs of operation are shared by the two users, but their use of the equipment need have nothing in com-

mon. Difficulties in scheduling may often be encountered. An alleviating factor, however, is that most of the bank's processing loads are centered on the night shift, whereas most industrial applications are handled during the day.

Some indication of the relative popularity of these four arrangements is given by the responses of 214 banks that utilize outside servicing.

Type of Service Used	Number of Banks	Per-Cent of Total
Cooperative centers	34	16
Correspondent banks	104	49
Service bureaus	56	26
Joint venture with nonbanks	7	3
Other	13	6
Total	214	100

In addition to outside servicing, two other trends in overcoming the economic obstacle to small-bank automation are evident. First, the development of lower-cost computers and "software," already noted, tends to lower the break-even point in terms of size and activity. A recent example is IBM's 1240, a cut-down sorter-reader with an equipment configuration designed to appeal to the smaller bank. Its promotional literature stresses the theme "For bankers who think they can't afford an MICR system." The second trend is to emphasize the computer's advantages in terms other than strictly cost-saving ones. These include a number of intangibles such as alleviation of personnel and supervision problems, more immediate control over operation, and more effective management information. The capability of the computer to broaden the scope and range of services offered by the automated bank is also frequently emphasized. This capability will be considered in some detail in the next chapter.

CONTROL AND AUDIT

Problems of auditing electronically processed accounting records for accuracy and reliability are being encountered by all business firms using computers. In commercial banking this is a major concern to both internal auditors and regulatory-agency examiners. The substitution of magnetic tapes for "hard," readable records was one of the major problems in determining the technical feasibility of bank automation.

Two quotations from Gregory and Van Horn, contrasting manual and EDP systems, will point up the auditing problem.

The small, discrete processing steps (in manual processing) are reflected in paper yielding a visual trail traceable in an unbroken path from start to finish. The large number of people working in the processing stream facilitates detecting and correcting errors made in earlier stages. . . . Responsibility for transactions, records and asset custody can be separated, and even atomized, to achieve checks and balances important to internal control. . . . [In EDP, on the other hand:] The commonly used media of punched cards, punched tape and magnetic tape are efficient for machine usage but not for people who want readable data. . . . Increasing the scope of processing runs and eliminating intermediate records, summaries, and analyses will modify or even obliterate the traditional audit trial connecting input and output. . . . Control over large volumes of data is now concentrated in the hands of a few people. . . . Many of the traditional checks and balances, whereby people at one stage have the opportunity to verify the work of others, may disappear.[11]

All these difficulties confronted the designers of automated bank systems and, in the early stages, presented an important obstacle to their acceptance. Completely satisfactory solutions have not been developed to date. Bank auditors, in common with all members of the profession, are actively exploring improved and more effective control measures. State and Federal Reserve examiners are confronted with the same problems. They have had to train, or add to their examining staffs, competent programmers and systems analysts. A sound understanding of the range of problems and the responses evolved to date may be gained by reference to the papers delivered to the ABA National Automation Conference.[12]

---

11. Gregory and Van Horn, *op. cit.*, p. 543, 544f.

12. American Bankers Association, *Proceedings, National Automation Conference* (New York, November 1963), pp. 99–119. The papers were as follows: Glenn M. Goodman (Assistant Director, Division of Examinations,

In addition to system design, banks have relied on the traditional safeguard of separating record-keeping and asset-handling functions. Many banks go a step further and separate programming and operating duties. Programmers are not permitted to run machine operations, and operators are kept out of programming. As in conventional banking operations, the clear-cut separation of functions is easy in large banks but presents a real problem to small banks that cannot afford it.

While audit and control present complicated problems in bank automation, most bankers agree that they have not proved to be major obstacles. Regulatory supervisors also take pride in the fact that examination problems have not dissuaded any bank that seriously wanted to automate.

MANAGEMENT ATTITUDE

Employee resistance to change is generally considered an important inhibiting factor in the adoption of technological change. Study of this area is beyond the scope of the present work; and no detailed investigation was made of employee attitude to automation. Only the opinions of bank officers who discussed the subject can be quoted here. Most bankers believed that very little opposition was evident among affected employees. They attributed this to two major factors: (1) employees were fully informed of automation plans and programs, and (2) the no-layoff-due-to-technology policy was almost unanimously adopted. Several bankers pointed out that developments might have been different had employees been represented by a single union or organization.

It might be pointed out here that a similar emphasis on the importance of keeping employees informed is suggested by a

Board of Governors of the Federal Reserve System), "What Examining Authorities Look For in the Computerized Bank"; John F. Sullivan (Supervising Bank Examiner, Banking Department, State of New York), "How to Meet Supervisory Needs in the Computerized Bank"; and Raymond C. Hubert (Manager, Systems and Procedures, The Boatmen's National Bank, St. Louis, Missouri), "Meeting a Bank's Internal Audit Needs Under Automation."

Department of Labor study of automation in the Internal Revenue Service.[13] On the other hand, Faunce, Hardin, and Jacobson's analysis found that employee morale in an insurance company installing a computer was not significantly affected by the extent to which employees were kept posted of changes planned.[14]

Although employee attitude was generally dismissed as inconsequential, the attitude of top management was frequently stressed as a major obstacle. The large majority of bank officers interviewed by the writer were in the upper levels of so-called "middle-management," many of them with a systems or computer orientation. These bankers felt there was a significant gap in the understanding of the true capabilities and potentials of automation by most banks' top managements. While senior bank officers could readily perceive the computer's ability to mechanize or speed up a variety of manual and bookkeeping operations, they could not visualize its more revolutionary capabilities in information processing and decision making.

The problem was succinctly stated by William F. Kelly, president of the American Bankers Association:

> One of the biggest and most important duties of operations officers is educating the rest of management on the basic concepts and capabilities of these electronic timesavers.[15] This is an entirely new field for most of us. Remember, almost all the people in bank management today were out of high school and college before the first computer ever went into operation. And, if any systems are going to work they must be understood and supported by everyone in management.[16]

Some of the younger operating officers believe that wholehearted adoption and exploitation of the computer's full potential

13. U.S. Department of Labor, Bureau of Labor Statistics, *Impacts of Office Automation in the Internal Revenue Service*, Bulletin No. 1364 (July 1963).

14. William A. Faunce, Einar Hardin, and Eugene H. Jacobson, "Automation and the Employee," *The Annals of the American Academy of Political and Social Science*, Vol. 340 (March 1962), pp. 60–68.

15. Note the perception of the computer as a "timesaver," even in this understanding view, by the president of a successfully automated bank.

16. ABA *Proceedings, op. cit.*, p. 35.

will not be possible before a new generation of managers takes over the highest levels of banking. Others feel that, with suitable education and "selling," even the current generation of top-level managers will fully accept and encourage greater automation. Both groups agree that a lack of enthusiasm and understanding by top managements is probably the major single obstacle to a more intensive exploitation of automation by the commercial banking system.

IV
Diversified Computer Applications— A Broad Range of Options

It was noted earlier that the diffusion of technological advances in any industry may be gauged along two dimensions. The "horizontal" proliferation of computer installations in an increasing number of banks was documented in Chapter II. An equally impressive penetration has been experienced in another dimension, namely, the intensity and diversity of exploitation of the new technology by each individual bank. This chapter will examine this "vertical" proliferation, its determinants, and its broad potential.

Horizontal proliferation is readily demonstrated by statistical tables or graphs showing the number or percentage of automated banks in successive time periods. A rapid rise in these numbers offers dramatic evidence of widespread diffusion. Vertical proliferation, on the other hand, is a far less spectacular process. It is almost impossible to quantify, in industry-wide terms, and it demands a more subtle evaluation than a mere nose count. Yet many bankers believe that in the long run the intensity with which the new technology is exploited will prove far more significant than its proliferation through a large number of banks.

There are, unfortunately, no data to indicate the number or variety of computer applications in banks in different time periods or stages of development. Even if current data were available, it would hardly indicate the rate at which vertical proliferation has progressed. The substantial delay in designing, testing, and implementing new computer applications was noted earlier. With the relative newness of most bank installations, it is more than likely that more applications were in the planning stage than in operation at the time of writing in 1964. That was certainly the case in the limited sample that the writer studied directly. The rate of vertical proliferation, would, therefore, tend to be grossly understated.

Despite these limitations, it may be stated positively that virtually no bank is content to use its computer for a single application. In every bank interviewed by the writer at least half a dozen applications were being made. A random examination of more than a hundred responses to the ABA survey questionnaire revealed that very few banks reported only a single computer application. Even these few stated they were then planning additional applications.

In its adoption of the new technology the banking system selected the general-purpose computer as the principal vehicle. In contrast to special-purpose or single-purpose computers, this hardware is extremely flexible. It can be programmed to perform an almost infinite range of data-processing tasks. An ABA bulletin to member banks titled "Suggested New Services Banks Can Offer with Computers" lists over ninety specific items under seventeen major classifications of banking operations.

In exercise of these options, banks almost universally selected demand-deposit accounting as the first computer application. No such unanimity of choice is evident in the selection of the second, third, or subsequent applications. As the number of applications adopted by each bank increases, the similarity of computer exploitation by different banks decreases. A conceptual explanation for this phenomenon will be developed in the next chapter. In preparation, however, it is necessary to examine the main forces responsible for vertical proliferation and the diversity of applications already in common use.

4.1. Principal Factors in the Diversification of Computer Applications

The following points summarize in six broad classifications the variety of factors—stated in many different forms—cited in interviews with bank officers and consultants.

1. Once a computer application has been installed and "proved out" in operation, its cost-saving capability is visibly demonstrated, and the advantages obtained for the first application are sought for other functions where problems of costs, employee availability, or mounting volume are acutely felt. Management gains closer familiarity with the new technology or, at the very least, some of its mystery is dissipated. Whatever success is achieved in one area is eagerly pursued in others.

2. The relatively high implementation costs of the initial installation and the continuing sizable expense of equipment rentals and operating staff present a powerful incentive for spreading such costs over as many applications as possible. Except in the extremely high-volume operations of the largest banks, demand-deposit accounting does not utilize the full capacity of the system installed. Additional applications can thus be implemented at comparatively small increases in marginal costs. Even in the busiest of installations, the need to balance work-flows, the ability to run peripheral equipment· off-line, and the need to have back-up capacity often result in available time on both the main computer and its auxiliary equipment. For some applications, additions to the peripheral equipment may be needed, but again these represent a relatively low marginal cost when compared to the sunk cost in other equipment, available personnel, and technicians. The argument of low marginal costs for new applications has even been advanced in cases where the addition of a complete equipment configuration was required. The sunk cost in such cases was represented by the skill, know-how, and competence acquired by staff officers, technicians, and operators in mastering the initial application. It should also be noted that

63

equipment rentals for other than prime-shift operation are normally 30 to 50 per cent lower; hence a two- or three-shift operation can substantially reduce the average hourly rental cost of an installation.

3. The existence of a group of computer-wise officers exerts yet another pressure for diversification of applications and services. Operating officers charged with the design and implementation of the initial application typically turn out to be zealous missionaries of the new technology. Aside from the desire to bring improvements to more bank operations, a number of more subjective incentives also develop. The innovators, who had relished the challenge of planning and designing a new system, find its routine operation far less exciting, and in some cases their coveted status as members of a hand-picked task force is threatened with dissolution. Almost all operating officers interviewed believed that their importance to the bank and their consequent status in the organization had been substantially increased with the conversion to computer processing. It is only natural then to find operating officers actively interested in increasing their bank's reliance on the computer—the new tool that they understand and, in varying degrees, control.[1]

In several banks permanent systems or systems research departments (similar to the Fidelity Bank and Trust department mentioned in Chapter III) have been established; their primary function is to analyze and develop new computer applications. In these cases there is a consistent and persevering force for diversification of computer services.

4. The active competition between banks for depositors and correspondents, as well as the competition between banks and other financial institutions, has provided a strong impetus for diversification of computer applications. This has resulted in the development of a number of services the bank can offer to its depositors and customers. As soon as any bank announces a new

---

1. Cf. Ida R. Hoos, *Automation in the Office* (Washington, D.C.: Public Affairs Press, 1961), pp. 18–20, on the "new office elite."

service to its customers, its immediate competitors must give serious consideration to offering a similar service or face the threat of losing customers to the innovating bank. Most officers agree that customers would not normally be lured away by a single service elsewhere, but they strongly feel that a sizable differential in the total services offered could result in a significant loss of customers. The tradition of broadening and improving the services offered customers certainly preceded the computer. Punched-card and tabulator installations served to expand many banks' range of customer services. Because of the greater flexibility of the computer, this trend shows every indication of accelerating.

5. Several new services made possible by the computer contain a built-in element for acquiring new depositors. For example, a sophisticated payroll service for an industrial customer, in which all employee accounts are electronically and directly credited, requires that each employee maintain a deposit account with the bank. Aside from the advantage of enlarging the number of depositors, the bank also enjoys considerable economies in handling costs. Electronic processing of the transaction bypasses the several paper exchanges that would otherwise be involved in issuing a pay check and then getting it back with a deposit slip. Similar advantages accrue to an Ohio bank, which under an arrangement with Blue Cross, debits its depositors accounts directly with the monthly or quarterly premiums for which they have contracted. As Blue Cross allows a 10 per cent discount on premiums collected by the bank, there is a tangible incentive for Blue Cross subscribers to open checking accounts. In addition, there is the less tangible advantage of added convenience for the depositor.

It is interesting to note that a number of bankers interviewed voiced their objections to the "captive depositor" feature of some computer services—but on two radically different grounds. One school of thought believes it is unfair to force an employee to open an account with a specific bank and that such coercion will cause resentment. The other equally strongly believes that a bank should be able to exercise complete freedom of choice in the depositors it accepts; any service that commits the bank to accept a specified group of depositors violates the bank's freedom of choice.

6. Several bank officers—particularly in the smaller banks interviewed—pointed out that new services, besides aiding in the competition for deposits, can be *sold* to customers and thus build up bank revenues. In this view, the computer installation offers a means of broadening the bank's "product line" of marketable services, and should be so exploited, particularly at a time when profit margins are slim and under constant pressure.

Spurred by the factors cited, most banks actively begin to seek additional applications as soon as earlier ones are installed and in operation. The range of choices is an extremely broad one. Computer applications run the gamut from relatively simple mechanization of check sorting to such esoteric problems as mathematical simulation of money market behavior or the solution of complex linear programming models for industrial clients. A few of the many applications in operation or being planned will be examined briefly in the next section.

4.2. An Overview of the Diversification of Computer Applications

As noted earlier, the number of tasks that can be computerized is potentially very high and covers a broad range of banking operations. Instead of setting forth a comprehensive list of such applications, we will confine our discussion to a number of applications, selected so as to (1) illustrate some of the most commonly offered services, and (2) indicate the wide variety and scope of the computer's capability.

Applications are placed in two commonly accepted categories, internal and external. The former refer to systems concerned with in-bank accounting and other functions; the latter consist of services provided to customers and other outside clientele.

INTERNAL APPLICATIONS

Proof and transit. Directed at mechanizing and automating the handling of checks between banks, or between banks and clearing houses, this involves the sorting of checks by transit routes, proof of incoming and outgoing batches of checks, and preparation of cash letters. It is a logical adjunct to automated demand-deposit accounting and insures that each check is MICR-encoded with its dollar amount. This application is most popular in areas where a majority of all checks are MICR-encoded and where most of the banks in the clearing arrangement operate computer installations.

Installment loans. Many applications for loan accounting are already in operation. Outstanding loan balances are updated as installment payments are made, delinquent payments are flagged, and service charges and penalties computed. This is primarily a mechanized bookkeeping operation. A more sophisticated application actually permits the computer to "decide" whether specific requests for loans should be granted or rejected. A specially written computer program compares a set of inputs from each loan application with an established set of criteria and recommends appropriate action—grant, reject, or use discretion. The writer is aware of at least one bank, with widespread branch operations, that uses this means of insuring sound and uniform standards for loan acceptance.

Mortgage loans. This application is similar in design and scope to installment-loan accounting, with the added complications of maintaining escrow accounts for real estate taxes, insurance, and so forth, and periodic problems of varying the amount of the monthly installment. A program for accepting or rejecting mortgage-loan applications is also feasible here.

Personal trust. This is also a comparatively simple application for maintaining asset record files and accounting for cash and asset transactions for each trust account maintained by the bank. The computer offers relief from the bulky files, delays in processing, and the high cost of double-entry bookkeeping. On the other hand, possibilities for much more sophisticated use of the computer in this area are currently being explored.

Bank payrolls. If the number of employees is large enough to warrant it, the computer provides a convenient way for processing the bank's own payroll. Output may be in the form of a pay check or direct account crediting. In addition, a variety of statistical and control reports may be obtained as a by-product. This application is also useful as a pilot operation for determining the feasibility of programs designed to process customers' payrolls, and it can also "debug" such a program. A somewhat more elaborate program, in banks where incentive payments are made to clerical employees, can compare actual payments with pre-set standards. Use of this program permits measuring and comparing the productivity achieved by individuals or departments. One application of this type is discussed in Chapter VI.

Variety of control data. Many internal applications can yield, as a by-product, information and reports for improving management control over bank operations. The productivity reports mentioned are a case in point. Similarly, important management information has been developed from demand-deposit accounting to tighten controls over customers' offsetting balances, the identification of uncollected funds in such balances, and the levels of activity and services rendered. Many applications of this type are commonly classified as "management information systems," a category which will be discussed more fully in Chapter V.

Market research and follow-up. This permits bank management to guide the efforts and evaluate the results of its business-development personnel. Coded data from census reports of each district's market potential are sorted in memory tapes by a number of relevant classifications. Periodic market-penetration reports are compared to the potential indicated for each geographic area or branch territory, the variations being used to select marketing strategy or appraise performance.

Money management and portfolio selection. This is a tantalizing area for bank managements, with many major problems yet to be solved but also with promise of great rewards. For the large banks with substantial deposits to invest the prospect of even a $\frac{1}{10}$ per cent improvement in yields—through higher investment returns or lower idle balances—can raise incomes by hundreds of thousands of dollars. Some intensive, but unpublicized, research is currently being carried out by a few large banks. IBM also has been developing a number of computer programs for applications in this area.

The computer's contribution to this area of bank management can be an extremely broad one. It can range all the way from performing relatively simple arithmetic computations (but in such profusion as to render the same problem insoluble by manual means) to the simulation of highly complex mathematical models. In the recently developed program for bond-trading analysis designed to determine when specific bonds in the bank's portfolio should be switched, the arithmetic involved is comparatively simple, but the number of computations needed rises sharply as the number of bonds to be compared increases.

There have been several attempts at developing a program to determine the best price to bid when a bond issue is put up at auction. Considerable mathematical sophistication is required if the program attempts to simulate both current and anticipated conditions in the money market. This type of computer use, with heavy reliance on operations research techniques, represents the most elaborate and complex set of internal applications currently being planned.

EXTERNAL APPLICATIONS

Internal applications made available to customers. Several of the applications listed as internal can be—and often are—offered to customers, correspondent banks, or other financial institutions. For example, demand-deposit accounting is frequently offered to correspondent banks; installment-loan accounting to correspondent banks and finance companies; mortgage-loan accounting to insurance companies and mortgage servicing companies; and payrolls and market-research data to any and all customers. The last two applications—payroll and market research—are in fact commonly considered to be external applications primarily, but which a bank may choose to employ internally.

Corporate trust. The two principal functions of corporate trust work—dividend paying and stock-transfer recording—have been performed successfully on punched-card installations by many of the large banks for many years. Computerizing the transfer record is usually warranted only if the number of stockholders is extremely high; otherwise, daily processing of large files with relatively low activity proves uneconomical on magnetic-tape equipment. The preparation of dividend checks, on the other hand, is a periodic activity in which every account number is involved and is therefore highly suited to computer processing. A program is generally written to compute the dividend amount for each stockholder and to print the dividend check. Portions of the same program may be readily used for proxy mailing, stockholders lists as of any given date, and address labels for annual statements or other corporate mailings. The Internal Revenue Service requirement that firms report all dividend payments has increased their work load but has also simplified the task in one important respect. A reporting number for each stockholder (required by the IRS) promises to solve the perennial problem of stockholder identification, since it substitutes a more precise identification than a name and address.

Accounting services for a variety of customers. Many accounting services are being offered or planned, depending on the nature or specialization of the community served by each bank. These include:

1. Insurance-company accounting—maintaining policy records on magnetic tape, preparing premium bills, and updating all policy records for premiums, claims, payments, and so forth. A single basic program can be modified to meet the needs of several insurance clients.

2. Department-store accounts receivable—to be maintained on magnetic tape, from which billing and invoicing, collection recording, and credit data can be processed for each customer.

7 0

3. Accounting services for small business—based on a standardized bookkeeping system that can develop periodic income statements and balance sheets in any degree of detail required by the customer.

4. Brokerage-firm accounting—a highly specialized program to maintain accounts and records for stockbrokers.

Clearly, a wide range of other accounting services may be offered to a great variety of customers. The common characteristic, typical of almost all customer services of this sort, is the size of the operation. It must be large enough to prove troublesome to the customer but not large enough to warrant the installation of a full-time computer system of his own. All these services can be processed during day shifts, when computer time is not critical for the bank's own needs and when equipment rental charges are substantially lower. These applications, however, all raise some question as to the extent of the processing bank's responsibility (or liability) for any errors in accounting or reporting—a question that still worries many bank officers. Despite the technical similarities of many of the services a bank may offer in this category, there are great individual differences in the manner in which these services must be merchandised. Some services may be offered directly to customers; others may be marketed best through the auditors or CPAs servicing the customer. The overall problems of merchandising external services, as well as the attempt to limit them by Federal legislation, are taken up in a subsequent section of this chapter.

Billing and collection services for a variety of customers. We have already mentioned the billing and collection services performed by banks for Blue Cross in Ohio. Similar services have been offered to local utility companies, municipal water systems, and others. Where direct-debiting of customer accounts is included as part of the system, the company saves not only the cost of preparing and mailing invoices but also any collection-agent's fees it may be paying. The customer can also anticipate faster cash flows as mailing delays are eliminated and the inevitably overlooked bill is no longer subject to the whims of the forgetful consumer.

Computational and operations-research services for customers. These are, by their very nature, highly specialized applications for each customer and type of service. Banks may keep inventory-control records for their industrial customers or run statistical-significance tests for their research clients. The bank's service may range from simply assigning computer time to the customer's technicians to use as they see fit to completely designing and writing the customer's programs. The second type of applications, however, require great skill in mathematical or scientific programming, usually totally unfamiliar to bank's programmers.

Some of the external applications discussed here lie in the area of traditional banking services, others are natural outgrowths of such services, but many are far removed from traditional bank functions. Speakers at the ABA National Automation Conference took diametrically opposite stands on the issue of which services properly belong in the bank's repertoire. At one extreme was the view that only direct banking functions should be undertaken and that even these be conservatively interpreted. At the other extreme, bankers viewed all traditional restrictions as outmoded; they held that any service, regardless of classification, that would improve a bank's competitive standing, increase its profits, or better serve its community, should be undertaken. The Waterbury National Bank in Connecticut, for example, is a firm believer in the latter point of view. It undertakes a wide range of services with little concern for their "banking" content. In contrast, the United States National Bank of Omaha has a check list that rigidly spells out seventeen criteria each contemplated service must meet before it will be offered by the bank.

4.3. Pricing of External Services

If the selection of appropriate external services proves perplexing to bank managements, the pricing of such services presents an even greater, and often more critical, problem. Bank services may be priced at whatever the traffic will bear, depending on the savings offered customers or on competitive prices set by outside service bureaus offering similar services. Or services may be given away free as a means of attracting depositors, correspondents, or other desirable customers; or services may be priced anywhere in between, at self-cost or self-cost plus some profit margin.

Pricing policy is usually set by top management and of necessity depends on the individual bank's competitive situation, relationship with its customers, and priority of objectives. It is doubtful if any reliable data is available or can be secured to indicate the number of banks favoring any given pricing policy. There is little doubt, however, that most bankers feel that too many costly external services are being offered free or are inadequately priced.

A further complication in pricing policy is the *manner* in which services are to be paid for. Bank services may be payable in cash or by the maintenance of offsetting balances. Offsetting balances are difficult to compute and to relate fairly to the many services a bank offers its customers, some of which may not even be listed as "services rendered." Another objection to offsetting balances is their varying marginal utility. The true value of an offsetting balance will vary from one bank to another, and even for the same bank at different times. Hence, rather than try to price services in units that have no common denominator and which are based on a sliding scale of values, many bankers feel that services should be paid for in cash.

Finally it should be pointed out that even with a pricing policy designed to recapture full costs and yield a profit, there are considerable practical difficulties in computing the correct price. Full costing of any service presents a major problem of fixed-cost allocations, determination of the incremental costs to be included, and the form in which prices are to be quoted. Conscientious pricing of external services often leads to a rather complex fee schedule. For example, in offering demand-deposit accounting to its correspondents, one bank's charges consist of (1) a charge per account serviced, (2) a charge per item processed, and (3) a minimum monthly or annual charge for each account carried. Fortunately, the computation of actual charges—once the fee schedule is programmed—presents little problem to the servicing bank. Charges are computed as a by-product of the processing of the customer's work, with only minor additions to set-up times or report preparations.

It should also be noted that if full-cost pricing is to be achieved, banks must embark on fairly elaborate market-research programs before any new service is adopted. They must make an estimate of the market potential for each contemplated service, estimate the customer's displaced costs (as a result of acquiring the new service), and ascertain the prices of competitive services or close substitutes for them. Only then can the bank weigh potential income against indicated costs. In some instances services that do not immediately promise to break even are adopted if forecasts of potential demand indicate a satisfactory rising trend within the next few years. Although such pricing problems have confronted most manufacturing companies for many years, they are relatively new to commercial banks. The price-cost relationship of bank services was of relatively small interest to bankers in prewar days when demand-deposit balances were large enough to permit the luxury of a variety of customer services without undue concern for their cost.

4.4. Marketing of External Services

The emergence of the new services made possible by the computer has placed new demands on banks' selling and merchandising functions. Commercial banks have always been active in selling their services and such selling has long been a major function of many bank officers. The sale of traditional bank services, however, primarily centered on maintaining sound and continuing relationships with customers. Bank officers were thoroughly familiar with their customers' banking requirements and with the range of services they could offer. As newer services are developed, however, it is increasingly difficult for the bank's credit officers to be familiar with their customers' specific needs in many areas of their business. It is even more difficult to possess the detailed technical knowledge required in explaining the advantages or evaluating the applicability of new services to customers. A new dimension of technical selling has of necessity been introduced in the business-development function of the bank seeking to diversify its computer-based services. The full force of this change is only just beginning to be felt by a small number of banks. Some banks have already added technicians to the sales force as others have formed new customer-service departments. It is already obvious, however, that we may anticipate significant impact on the sales function, where heavy reliance will be placed on external, technically oriented customer services.

If bankers, or other computer users, ever doubted that the expansion of external services could bring about far-reaching changes in the banking system, these doubts must have been dispelled by recent opposition to such expansion. On December 20, 1963, a bill was introduced by Congressman Abraham Multer "to prohibit banks from performing certain nonbanking services."[2] This bill was aimed at all national banks, all members of the Federal Reserve System, and all banks insured by the Federal Deposit Insurance Corporation. These three categories encompass with minor exceptions the entire commerical banking system of the United States. The bill proposed the following:

No bank [as defined in the foregoing paragraph] may perform any clerical, administrative, bookkeeping, statistical, accounting, or other similar services for its depositors, borrowers, or other customers, except to the extent that such services are a necessary incident to the proper discharge of lawful functions of such bank as a depository, lender, trustee, or agent.

At the time of writing, in 1964, the Committee on Banking and Currency was considering the bill. Should this bill be adopted

---

2. U.S. Congress, House, 88th Cong., 1st Sess., 1963, H.R. 9548.

into law, it will drastically alter the banking system's approach to external services.[3] Its very introduction, however, points up the potential impact of an expanding range of bank services. The adoption of computer technology and hardware by the banks is obviously thought to place the banking system in direct competition with nonbanking firms and institutions. The fact that the Association of Data Processing Service Organizations (ADAP-SO) and several CPA organizations are among the most active supporters of the proposed bill identifies some of the major areas in which bank competition is anticipated.

---

3. Updating note, to December 1966. In the current session of Congress, Congressman Abraham Multer of Brooklyn, New York, introduced two bills (H.R. 112 and H.R. 10529) designed to accomplish essentially the same objectives as his earlier bill. Subcommittee hearings have been held, but no report has been published as of the time of going to press.

V

The Process of Automation—
A Conceptual View

Automation, or indeed any technological advance, is generally viewed as the utilization of certain hardware or techniques in a firm's operations. Banks are "automated" when they install an electronic digital computer; an automobile-engine plant is "automated" when automatic work-feeding devices are introduced between a series of transfer machines.[1] This direct relationship between technological advance and its hardware has led to a rather simple-minded view of the process of automation: a firm is automated when it acquires certain machinery or equipment; it becomes "more automated" when it installs bigger machines or uses the same machines in a greater part of its operations.

A considerably more sophisticated view recognizes *levels* of automation or mechanization. In Bright's words,

The concept of levels of mechanization is based on the assumption that there are different degrees of mechanical accomplishment in machinery. In what way does machinery supplement man's muscles, his senses, his mental processes, and his judgement? Are there significant differences in responsiveness of machinery? What characterizes them?[2]

Bright proceeds to identify seventeen levels of mechanization. These range from hand operations (level 1) through power tool

1. Bright, *Automation and Management*, p. 5.
2. *Ibid.*, p. 41.

system, remote controlled (level 7) to anticipating required performance and adjusting accordingly (level 17). Using these levels, Bright develops the concept of a mechanization profile and plots such profiles for several companies in a variety of industries.[3] In a similar approach, Amber and Amber identify ten levels in what they call "order of automaticity."[4] These are numbered A_0 through A_9 and range from hand tools and manual machines (A_0), through self measuring and adjusting (A_4), to commands others (A_9).

This approach, still centered on the hardware in use, is extremely helpful to the engineer or technician. Its usefulness to the manager, however, is severely limited. These concepts may help explain differences between different industries using a variety of machines and processes, but they do little to conceptualize the experiences of a single industry's adoption of a relatively homogeneous combination of hardware. The case study of bank automation leaves a number of important questions unanswered.

The electronic computer, as a piece of technological hardware, must be ranked at a rather high level of mechanization or "order of automaticity." On the Amber and Amber scale it would probably rate an A_7 or A_8. It is somewhat more difficult to place it on Bright's scale, which is focused on production machinery rather than data processing. Even there, however, a rating around level 13 would seem appropriate. Yet when the computer's actual use is examined, a substantially lower rating must be assigned in many instances. Many banks, for example, employ their computers in applications that would rate no higher than level 5 or A_2—power tool, fixed cycle, or single-cycle automatics, respectively. Does it then make sense to view automation in terms of the capability of the hardware involved? Or is the level at which this hardware is actually exploited more significant?

If the second questioned is answered by "yes"—which certainly

---

3. *Ibid.,* pp. 46–55.
4. George H. Amber and Paul S. Amber, *Anatomy of Automation* (Englewood Cliffs, New Jersey: Prentice-Hall, Inc., 1962), Chapter I.

seems more logical—why do we find differing levels of automation exploited by different banks in the system? Why is there great uniformity in the first application or two and equally great diversity in subsequent applications?

Does the addition of applications to any bank's repertoire represent a steady and continuing rise in the level of automation? The empirical evidence refutes this contention. A relatively low-level application is often introduced *after* much higher-level ones. Is it reasonable then to say that a bank has become "more automated" as a result of the latest application?

Perhaps the area of most interest to the manager is the one concerned with the *impacts* of automation. Will differences in levels of automation fully serve to explain—and eventually predict—its impact? The four case studies presented in the following chapter strongly suggest that the answer is "no."

In order to provide some answers to these questions, we must focus attention on the actual exploitation of the new technology, rather than on the capabilities of its hardware. Furthermore, it is important to consider not only *how* the technological advance is exploited—as conceptualized by a level of automation—but also for *what* purpose. In the approach suggested here we recognize the close association between automation and its hardware but have modified our view of the latter. Automation's hardware—the computer, in our case—is viewed as a bundle of capabilities. The process of automation is seen as the progressive exploitation of these capabilities by a firm.

The computer's bundle of capabilities may be analyzed along several dimensions: engineering, economic, and even social. For the manager it is most meaningful to discuss capabilities in terms that relate to the firm's broad objectives and its operations. Our analysis will be restricted to three such dimensions. This will give us the added advantage of being able to represent our findings graphically. Computer capabilities will be treated along three axes: two will describe the *direction* taken by automation and the third will define its operational *level*. The two directional axes are closely related to major firm objectives—cost reduction and revenue production. The third is closely analogous to the "levels of automation" suggested by Bright.

The validity of cost reduction and revenue production as significant dimensions of technological advance is confirmed by John Maurice Clark's discussion of innovation in general.

> We may focus our discussion around initiatory or aggressive innovations made in the hope of increased profits, with the understanding that the inducement to defensive innovations on the part of competitors seeking to avoid a reduction of profits or to minimize deficits acts with even more compelling force. *Larger profits per unit may come from a reduction of costs,* either from more economical processes of producing the same commodity or from cost reducing alterations in the product. . . . The second major method of increasing a firm's total profits is *to increase its dollar volume of sales,* either by price reductions, which may be made possible by reduced costs, or by making its product attractive to more buyers, or through increased total selling effort, including entering new geographical market areas or tapping new strata of demand. . . .
>
> These ways of utilizing an innovation to increase profits may be employed in almost any kind of combination.[5]

Similarly, in a direct reference to the benefits of automated data processing, Gregory and Van Horn state: "The benefits that accrue from information and decisions are reduced costs or increased revenues throughout an organization."[6]

A word of explanation should be offered about each of the analytical axes we shall use.

The cost-reducing capability can be exploited directly (for example, a reduction of six clerks in Department A), or indirectly (for example, lowering Department A's turnover rate from 50 per cent to 30 per cent, thereby reducing hiring and training costs). It can also be exploited at different levels of automation, as presently defined. Cost reduction is probably the capability most commonly associated with any advance in mech-

---

5. John Maurice Clark, *Competition as a Dynamic Process* (Washington, D.C.: The Brookings Institution, 1961), pp. 199–200. The italics are this author's.

6. Gregory and Van Horn, *Automatic Data-Processing Systems,* p. 141.

80

anization or automation, but all too often it is treated as the sole capability.

The revenue-producing capability is exploited, as its name implies, in increasing the firm's gross income. As Clark noted, such exploitation can be achieved in a variety of ways. In bank automation it is achieved principally either by the sale of new services made possible by the computer, or by the raising of incomes and yields through improved asset and service management. The two approaches generally imply exploitation at different automation levels.

Although both cost reduction and revenue production are direct determinants of a firm's profit margin, they are by no means the reciprocals of each other. Cost-reducing applications need add nothing to revenues; revenue production may actually increase costs. The pursuit of either objective entails a very different set of efforts and typically creates a markedly different set of impacts.

The operational level of automation is a somewhat modified version of the concept suggested by Bright. Instead of seventeen levels primarily concerned with the *mechanical* features of the system, only three levels will be identified, and these will focus on the *operational* capability of the system. The three levels are thus still treated as capabilities of the new technology, with a continuum of gradations within each level.

Level I—the capability to improve existing services. "Improve" may have a variety of meanings: to lower costs, to take in greater revenues, to improve accuracy, to achieve faster response, and so forth. Such improvement, however, applies to services already offered and performed by the firm. The gradations within this level are somewhat analogous to the approaches to systems design suggested by Gregory and Van Horn, discussed in Chapter III. At the lower extreme—simplification and mechanization—lie those applications that merely speed up or mechanize existing procedures. The same basic operations are still performed with little or no change in information flows, inputs, or outputs. At the upper extreme, an existing service is still performed, but the systems and procedures involved in its performance are drastically altered. Some operations may be eliminated altogether; others, radically changed in terms of information flows, inputs, and outputs.

Level II—the capability to introduce new services. Automation enables firms to expand their product, or service, line. There are gradations within this level also. At the lower extreme are those services that, although new for a particular bank, have long been regarded as traditional banking functions. At the upper extreme lie radically different services not normally associated with the banking system. Check-account reconciliation is an example of the former; solution of engineering problems, an example of the latter.

Level III—the capability to simulate management decision making. At this level the computer is used as a relatively sophisticated brain, rather than a replacement of hands and eyes. In this sense, levels I and II describe the computer's *operational* capability, whereas level III represents its *managerial* or decision-making capability. A similar distinction between this level and the two preceding ones is made by Melvin Anshen.

> The new information technology enters the world of management in two ways. The first is marked by the use of powerful computers in processing masses of data previously handled by clerks using pencil calculations and simple machines with slow speed and limited capacity. The second is marked by the application of sophisticated techniques of quantitative analysis, both old and new, to management problems.[7]

Computer applications within this level are usually given the generic name of "management-information systems"—an extremely fashionable, if vaguely defined term, in computer circles. The writer was subjected to a multitude of definitions, the most effective of which smacks heavily of circular reasoning. Applications on this level deal with the kinds of problems handled by the manager, rather than the clerk or operator. Gradations within this level can then be related to the hierarchy of management

---

7. Melvin Anshen, "Managerial Decisions," *Automation and Technological Change* (Englewood Cliffs, New Jersey: Prentice-Hall, Inc., 1962), p. 70.

levels involved in each application. Somewhat more rigorously, gradations may be related to Herbert Simon's scale of programmed versus nonprogrammed decisions.[8] The more nonprogrammed, the higher the gradation level. It should be noted here that truly comprehensive management-information systems require highly sophisticated, large-capacity hardware, comparable to the IBM 7090, for example. Equipment of this level of sophistication is only just being introduced to commercial banking.

Finally it should be pointed out that no sharp demarcation lines between levels exist in practice. Some overlap, and subjective judgment is inevitable in any classification system.

Similarly, the gradations within levels represent a continuum rather than a series of discrete steps, as Simon points out.

Having christened them, I hasten to add that they are not really distinct types, but a whole continuum. . . . We can find decisions of all shades of gray along the continuum, and I use the terms programmed and nonprogrammed simply as labels for the black and the white of the range.[9]

5.1. Graphic Representation of Computer Applications

Having thus established three axes of computer capability, they may now be used to define graphically a three-dimensional exploitation space. The two axes along the horizontal plane will represent the cost-reducing and revenue-producing capabilities. The vertical axis will indicate the level of exploitation. As our main purpose is to develop a conceptual framework, no attempt will be made to establish quantitative scales along the horizontal axes. In principle, these could be scaled in dollar volumes, representing absolute amounts of lowered costs or increased earnings. Or, if it is desirable to plot banks of varying sizes within a com-

8. Herbert A. Simon, *The New Science of Management Decision* (New York: Harper & Row, 1960), p. 5.
9. *Ibid.*

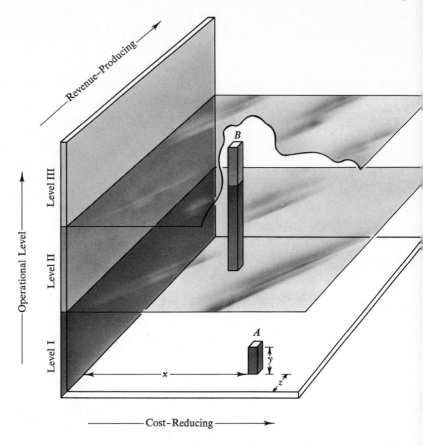

Figure 5.1—Graphic Representation of Two Computer Applications

parable graphic space, relative scale units may be used—for example, percentages of preautomation costs and revenues.

Within the exploitation space defined by the three axes, computer applications can be depicted by upright columns. (See Figure 5.1.) Each column indicates the extent to which each dimension of capability is exploited by the application it represents. For example, the computer application represented by column A exploits each of the technology's three capabilities, as indicated by the following dimensions. The column's horizontal distance (x) from the origin represents its exploitation of the cost-reducing capability. Its depth (z) from the frontal plane represents its revenue-producing content. While its height (y) represents the level of automation exploited. Ignoring its relatively minor z-dimension, application A could be broadly described as a cost-reducing mechanization of an existing service. By contrast, the application represented by column B is the introduction of a new revenue-producing, non-traditional banking service. (Note that column B height extends well into level II.)

The primary usefulness of the three-dimensional analysis proposed here is not, however, in locating any particular application's position in the exploitation space. Rather, the analysis is useful in viewing the process or dynamics of computer utilization in any one bank. The *movement* in this three-dimensional space is of primary interest.

5.2. *The Concept of the Exploitation-Path*

The process by which a firm exploits the capabilities of a new technology can be illustrated graphically by plotting the successive applications to which the new technology is put. Consider, for example, the progressive steps involved in a typical bank's automation process.

In common with the general practice, our hypothetical bank embraces automation by computerizing its demand-deposit accounting. It now stands at step 1 in Figure 5.2, that is, it mainly exploits the computer's cost-reducing ability (by a reduction in its bookkeeping personnel); it achieves a minor increment in revenue-production (by collecting some additional service charges that were formerly overlooked in manual processing); and it utilizes its equipment at a relatively low level of automation (check sorting and posting have been mechanized with only minor changes in information flows).

Our bank next converts its savings-deposit accounting to com-

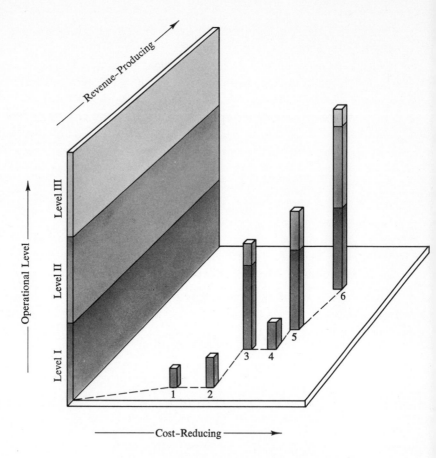

**Figure 5.2—Successive Applications in a
Bank's Automation Program**

puter processing and thereby moves to step 2 in the diagram.
The movement has been entirely along the cost-reducing axis,
resulting from a further reduction in clerical personnel. There
has been no further exploitation of the revenue-producing capability, hence no movement inward, away from the frontal plane.
The level of the new application is, however, a little higher. Not
only has bookkeeping been mechanized, but a change in processing has also been introduced. Savings pass books were eliminated

and tellers need no longer post and update these for each deposit or withdrawal.

As its next step (step 3), our bank begins to sell demand-deposit accounting to its correspondents. The introduction of this service makes no additional use of the cost-saving capability but does exploit the revenue-producing and diversification-of-services capabilities of the computer. Diagrammatically, therefore, the movement is inward and upward. Not that the height of column 3 places it in the lower portion of level II. A new service is added to our bank's repertory, but it is a relatively traditional one, the servicing of a correspondent.

Step 4 represents the computerizing of installment-loan accounting. The movement in the horizontal plane is toward further exploitation of the cost-reducing capability (a reduction in clerical personnel). The height of column 4 is approximately the same as that of column 2. An existing service is automated, with some change in operating procedures. Not only is the bookkeeping mechanized but borrower's coupon books are eliminated, and borrowers who are also depositors are given the option of having their installments paid by an automatic debiting of their checking account.

Our bank now begins to process and collect accounts receivable for two of its department-store depositors. This application is represented by column 5. The movement between steps 4 and 5 is, again, inward and upward. Revenue production and diversification of services are both exploited. Column 5 is higher than column 3, to reflect the fact that department-store accounting is a less traditional banking service than the servicing of correspondents.

Finally, our bank begins to manage its portfolio of government bonds by using a computer program designed to select advantageous shifts in bond holdings. As a result it is able to increase portfolio yields by, for example, ¼ per cent annually. Our bank is now at step 6 in the diagram. The movement from step 5 to 6 has been only slight, in the cost-reducing direction (minor savings in the clerical time needed to compute yields from

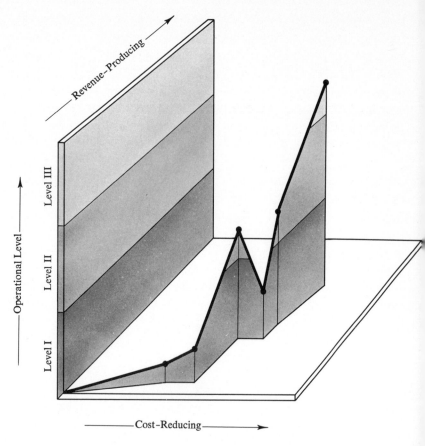

Figure 5.3—The Exploitation Path

coupon rates at varying market prices). There is, however, a substantial increase in the revenue-producing benefit represented by the ¼ per cent increase in yields. There is also a marked increase in the height of column 6. The computer's decision-making capability is now being exploited. Decisions formerly made by investment officers are now, at least partially, assigned to the computer. Column 6 reaches the lower range of level III.

The six-step program outlined here is probably sufficient to explain the proposed method for charting the series of applications installed in any bank's automation program. It only remains for us to indicate the evolutionary or dynamic nature of such a program by the integration of the six steps into a continuous path. Graphically, this is readily achieved by connecting the tops of the six columns plotted earlier, to yield the ramp-like diagram shown in Figure 5.3. The upper surface of this ramp is the "exploitation-path" traced by our model bank in its automation program. The round dots astride the path indicate applications actually exploited. At any stage of the process the path concept serves to point up both "where we stand" and "how we got there," in terms of the new technology's three basic capabilities. Exploitation-paths can thus be drawn for any individual bank, using the concepts and procedures described.

In applying the concept of the exploitation-path to our case study of bank automation, a number of important questions arise. What determinants shape the path traced by each individual firm? Will exploitation-paths be identical—or nearly so—for all firms in an industry? Will the impact of the new technology depend on the exploitation-path? These questions will be considered in the remainder of this chapter and in the next two.

5.3. The Determinants of a Firm's Exploitation-Path

We must first attempt to understand the factors that determine the shape of the exploitation-path traced by any firm. On a purely mechanical level the answer is quite simple. The exploitation-path is determined by the choice and sequence of applications installed by the firm's management. These management decisions, however, are not made in a vacuum. In selecting each computer application, the firm's management is confronted by a variety of internal and environmental forces and constraints. Some of these will favor cost-reducing applications; others will encourage revenue production. Similarly, some will encourage improvement of existing services; other will want to diversify the firm's service line.

Using our study of bank automation and the economic, institutional, and technical factors discussed in the preceding chapters, we shall consider the determinants of exploitation-path patterns in terms of several analytical axes. We shall analyze the manner in which such factors as competition, location, bank size, and so forth, affect the shape of the exploitation-path traced by each firm. Our analysis will progress from determinants that affect the commercial banking system as a whole to those that apply specifically to individual banks.

HISTORICAL MOMENTUM

The combination of forces and developments (described in Chapter II), which first focused bankers' attention on the new technology, played a major role in determining the shape of most banks' exploitation-paths. It will be recalled that the computer was first perceived as a cost-reducing device, a replacement for human hands and eyes. Bankers sought out operations that would yield maximum cost savings, while hardware manufacturers developed the peripheral equipment that could yield these savings. The momentum of the historical developments that introduced automation to banking thus tended to encourage early exploitation of the cost-reducing capability at relatively low level-I applications.

This is not to imply that the historical momentum behind all technological advances channels their exploitation in the cost-reducing direction. The development of nylon, for example, was not pursued as a low-cost substitute for natural fibers. Rather, the revenue-producing potential of a new product with certain superior properties guided and shaped this advance. Historical momentum is the combined result of many factors. In this sense it is itself a product of other determinants, some of which will be examined below.

INSTITUTIONAL CHANGES IN BANKING

The changing financial habits and practices, of both individuals and corporations since World War II, also tended to put primary emphasis on the exploitation of the cost-reducing capability of the computer. The revenue-producing capability received comparatively minor attention. From the case study presented in Chapter II we may draw a number of generalizations concerning institutional changes as determinants of the exploitation-path.

Firms will tend to pursue and exploit the cost-reducing capability of automation (1) when the volume of items to be processed manually—or by conventional means—has been growing at a rapid rate and the industry's projections indicate a continuing (or rising) growth trend; (2) when the number of outlets per processing organization (in this case, branch offices per bank) increases so that the firm must service a greater number of points of contact with its customers, suppliers, and public; (3) when the frequency and/or quality of servicing increases, so that the firm must perform more numerous or more costly services for its customers in its normal "line of duty"; (4) when operating costs show a rising trend as a result either of rising wage and salary levels in the industry at large or of specific operational conditions in a given department or function (for example, excessive labor turnover, hiring, or training costs).

Banks will also exploit the cost-reducing capability (5) when the firm becomes concerned with the growing *number,* quite aside from the cost, of personnel in troublesome areas of its operations (excessive number of employees foreshadows difficulties in recruiting, training, and supervising competent personnel; it also implies growing administrative complications, fringe benefits, and potential sources of friction and conflict); and (6) when resistance to cost-reducing measures is expected to be minimal. In our case study the no-layoff policy made possible by high turnover rates, as well as the absence of organized employee representation, resulted in little or no resistance to change.

All the factors cited above emphasize cost reduction via mechanization or substitution of the factors of production. As such, they encourage exploitation of the computer at level I. Comparatively little incentive is presented for exploitation at levels II and III.

Among the institutional changes discussed in Chapter II, only two factors directed bankers' attention to the revenue-producing capability of the new technology.[10]

1. Government regulations that restricted commercial banks' underwriting activities generated not only resistance to the restriction but also an active search for compensating sources of revenue. This search encouraged exploitation of the computer's revenue-producing capability at level II. It can be assumed that the same pattern would result from the restriction of the effectiveness of traditional services by constraints other than those of the government. Changes in social, moral, or political values may also render traditional services (or products) obsolete and, consequently, generate a search for substitutes.

2. The change in the commercial bank's image, with its closer relationship to the small depositor and the retail public, also encouraged the exploitation of new revenue-producing services. It did so by loosening the constraint inherent in the notion of traditional banking services. A broader view of what constitutes proper and respectable banking services permits a more comprehensive, less constrained search for new revenue-producing applications.

TECHNICAL CHARACTERISTICS

The principal piece of hardware in bank automation is the general-purpose digital computer. Its technical characteristics are, perhaps, the principal determinants for the continuous extension of the exploitation-path—in any direction. These technical

---

10. It should be hastily added that competition, which could well be treated as an institutional factor, was a major determinant in the exploitation of the revenue-producing capability. Because of its importance, however, competition is treated as a separate heading in our analysis.

characteristics make it almost certain that no firm's management will be content to consider its automation program complete with only one or two applications in operation.

Although the cost-reducing capability first attracted bankers' attention, the computer—when adopted—represented an inseparable bundle of all three capabilities. Thus, one of the principal factors directing management's attention to the computer's revenue-producing and higher-level capabilities was simply that, like Mount Everest, "it was there." This total bundle of capabilities and other technical characteristics of the computer spurred extensive exploitation of the new technology in a number of specific ways.

1. The relatively high implementation costs provided a powerful incentive for spreading these costs over as many applications as possible. The same thing is perhaps better stated in economic, rather than accounting, terms. Once installed (for the processing of any application) the computer represents substantial sunk costs. The introduction of additional applications involves comparatively minor incremental costs, often negligible when compared with the anticipated returns. Successive computer applications are therefore relatively easily justified on economic grounds. In an even broader sense the training, experience, and know-how developed in a bank's operations personnel may be viewed as a sunk cost, all further reduce the incremental costs associated with more extensive computer exploitation.

2. Bankers' reliance on general-purpose, stock-produced hardware enabled the equipment manufacturer to play a key role in extending computer exploitation. The manufacturers' contribution is evident in at least four areas.

a. They have developed lower-priced, higher-speed equipment that enhances the cost-versus-returns calculus on which the decision to automate is principally based. The initial effect is generally to encourage exploitation of the cost-reducing capability of the improved hardware. However, the computer's additional capabilities are made available at the same time.

b. They have developed improved "software," particularly

standardized programming and compilers. These not only reduce implementation costs but, even more significantly, enable banks to exploit capabilities that demand a greater technological sophistication than is generally available within the organization. This contribution of the manufacturer encourages a high level of exploitation by the firm. It permits relatively small banks, with few specialized EDP personnel, to exploit applications on levels II and III. A recent example is IBM's Bond Trade Analysis program for its 1401—a popular computer in bank installations.[11]

c. The computer manufacturers, with no small measure of enlightened self-interest, have assumed a vital role as carriers of the new technology. Besides offering highly specialized training programs for their customer's personnel, they have promoted, explained, and popularized office automation to bankers and the public. By dispelling the mysteries of EDP they have contributed to the education of top management throughout the industry. The gap in management's understanding is considered by many technicians as a major constraint on the exploitation of computer technology—or, at least, exploitation beyond the relatively simple and intuitively understood levels of mechanization and factor substitution.

d. Finally, by making the hardware available on a rental basis as well as by outright purchase the manufacturers helped alleviate one of the major constraints on the adoption of a rapidly developing technology—the fear of obsolescence. Sunk costs are thus lowered, and the exchange of hardware is not precluded if it is technologically obsolete before it is fully amortized.

3. We must note one more technical characteristic that encourages the exploitation of higher levels of capability, particularly at level III. Whereas applications at level I generally yield benefits proportional to the *volume* processed (machine runtime), there need be no such relationship at level III. As long as the computer is used as a production machine, the longer it runs

---

11. Cf. *General Information Manual: Bank Investment Portfolio* (White Plains, New York: International Business Machine Corporation, 1964).

the greater its benefit—in terms either of reduced costs or of increased revenues. Machine capacity thus becomes a limiting factor on the total benefits that may be reaped from the system. Management information applications (level III), on the other hand, can yield substantial advantages with comparatively short machine runs. An impressive increase in bond yields, for example, may be obtained by a portfolio-analysis program that takes only a few minutes of computer time. Thus, as level-I and level-II applications begin to strain equipment capacity, there is a strong incentive to exploit level-III applications without significantly adding to machine run-times.

COMPETITION

Competition, both interindustry and intraindustry, is an important determinant of the shape of the exploitation-path traced by each bank. We will first examine interindustry competition, between banks and other financial institutions, and then proceed to intraindustry competition within the commercial banking system.

INTERINDUSTRY COMPETITION

The aggressive and successful competition between the commercial banking system and other financial institutions was noted in Chapter II. This competition encouraged the exploitation of the computer's cost-reducing capability primarily for the two reasons noted earlier. It made it essential for banks to increase the frequency and quality of servicing to retain its traditional customers. The main thrust of interindustry competition, however, was to direct exploitation toward the revenue-producing capability.

An interesting example was reported to the writer at one large city bank. This bank's officers were extremely anxious to offer an improved installment-loan package recently developed by the commercial banks to compete with personal finance plans offered by other institutions. Under the bank's plan a depositor is granted a predetermined amount of credit. He may draw on it as needed simply by writing a check, or a series of checks, in payment for any purchases made. Repayment can be made, in whole or in part, at any time; this in effect creats a revolving credit—up to a given sum—for each approved borrower. This plan has been variously dubbed "Ready-credit" or "check-credit" by its sponsoring banks, and it is occasionally referred to wryly as "instant money."

The bank officials in question, although anxious to offer such a plan of their own, were keenly aware of the substantial book-keeping costs involved in controlling and computing interest charges on the large number of transactions it might involve. The top management's decision was to offer the new service only if its processing could be programmed for computer operation. A satisfactory computer program was developed, and the plan is now included in the package of banking services offered to the public. This is a clear example of a bank's exploitation of a new income-producing service, which was made possible by the availability of the new technology. The bank's interest in introducing the new service was, in turn, spurred by the active competition of other financial institutions.

The generalization that may be drawn is the rather obvious one that when the traditional services (or products) of a firm or an industry fail to maintain a share of the market in the face of competition from other industries, the firm or industry will intensify its search for new or competitive revenue-producing services (or products) made possible by technological innovation. Our case study of the banking system, however, indicates that we can proceed one step further in this generalization. We already noted that in response to external competitive pressures banks accepted—and even encouraged—a shift in the ratio of demand to time deposits, despite the higher cost of the latter. Thus it is that a firm will search actively for new revenue-producing services in the face of competition, even if the new services entail higher costs than those of the more traditional services that have been threatened by competition. This point also illustrates the relative independence in goal-seeking represented by the exploitation of the cost-reducing and revenue-producing capabilities of technological change. As in every other application of elementary microeconomics, a marginal decrease in the cost-reducing dimension will be accepted, if the resultant marginal increase in the revenue-producing dimension promises to be greater. Interindustry competition thus spurs exploitation of revenue-producing, level-II applications.

A by-product of higher-cost services made necessary by competition is the creation of an incentive for even higher levels of exploitation. If banks have to pay interest on a growing percentage of their deposits, they must earn higher yields on their assets. The new technology, if exploited at level III, offers bankers a means of meeting this requirement.

On the other hand, competition from nonfinancial institutions represents a constraint on banks' ability to exploit new revenue-producing applications, particularly at the higher ranges of level II. Data-processing services offer stiff competition to banks seeking to introduce new services not traditionally associated with commercial banking. The proposed bill to limit banks' EDP services is but a formal manifestation of this competitive constraint.

INTRAINDUSTRY COMPETITION

This form of competition, like the one just discussed, tends to put primary stress on revenue production and level-II exploitation. It does provide some incentive for cost reduction too. The correlation coefficients computed in Chapter III indicate that banks of approximately equal size incur similar costs in rendering traditional banking services. It was also noted that these services do not appear significantly different to bank depositors. Under these conditions, the cost reductions through automation made by one bank will place a competitive strain on other banks in its trading area to reduce their costs in a similar manner.

More important, however, is the tendency of competition to

stimulate the exploitation of level-II applications, whether or not they are directly motivated by additional revenue production. Competing banks often find it necessary to offer as complete a range of services to both depositors and correspondents as their most aggressive competitor offers. The fees charged for such services represent an increment in bank revenues and, as such, exploitation of the computer's revenue-producing capability. Often, however, the exploitation of this capability is not a conscious or premeditated one. It is a by-product of the bank's attempt to retain or attract depositors, and is not made to increase the range of services from which it can collect revenues. In extreme cases this dimension of exploitation may actually be decried or resented. One bank officer told the writer: "This customer payroll processing is a pain in the neck. We'd rather forego the few bucks we make on it than run it. But the other banks are offering it, so we've got to go along."

In a highly competitive industry such as banking, the tendency is to push computer exploitation to increasingly higher stages of level II. The scope of services that banks regard as appropriate is continuously expanded by the behavior of the most aggressive competitor. As J. M. Clark notes, it takes only one firm—even in a highly concentrated market—to introduce innovation into an entire industry.[12] Thus, although payroll processing was not viewed as a common banking service in the late 1950's, it is fast gaining this status in the automated bank.

Finally, aggressive competition between banks stimulates exploitation of level III of computer capability. Stated simply, competition enhances the need for better management and improved decision-making. Three brief references will suffice to illustrate this need. (1) Competitive bidding for municipal-bond underwriting has spurred the development of computer programs for bid preparation. (2) Competition for depositors has led some banks into highly sophisticated market-research programs for evaluating deposit potentials. (3) Competition for small-loan

---

12. Clark, *op. cit.*, pp. 202–207 and p. 481.

borrowers stimulated the development of a computer program to approve or reject loan applications. This is a task generally assigned to highly experienced officers or, at the risk of losing many sound loans, is guided by a few rigid limitations that could be applied by relatively unskilled personnel.

INTRAINDUSTRY COOPERATION

Mutual interest has also served in several ways to stimulate computer exploitation—primarily its cost-reducing capability.

We have already noted the contribution of a strong and competent industry association, the ABA, to the development of a common machine language. This standardization permitted the development of lower-cost equipment and prepackaged programming.

The unifying effects of the Federal Reserve System and its clearinghouses also proved a powerful force in exploiting the cost-reducing capability. The Federal Reserve's pressure to have all banks MICR-encode their checks has lowered the incremental cost associated with automated demand-deposit accounting. In more general terms, any industry-wide pressure to have all member firms contribute in some way to the adoption of a technological advance tends to encourage each firm to exploit the cost-reducing capability of this advance. This is an effective means of offsetting the added cost of the firm's contribution. Such contribution may be in the form of adherence to accepted standards of behavior, the supplying of new or additional information to the industry-wide system, or a change in the format or content of the firm's own records or procedures. Each of these elements was present in bank automation.

Cooperation within the banking system also encouraged exploitation of cost-reducing applications by lowering customer resistance to change. Many depositors at first objected to the redesign of their personal checks or were reluctant to receive statements any time except the end of a calendar month. Such opposition was generally overcome by the educational and promotional drive of the banking system, as well as by the united stand taken by competing banks in insisting on the need for procedural revisions.

Thus, industry cooperation primarily encourages exploitation of cost-reducing, level-I applications. Little, if any, stimulation is provided for exploitation at levels II and III. Insofar as the ABA serves as a clearninghouse of information and banks interchange some know-how, cooperation may assist some banks to install higher-level applications. As we shall see later, however, there appears to be a trend to restrict the free flow of information concerning level-III applications. This tendency is in sharp contrast to the prevailing "no secrets" policy on low-level applications.

BANK SIZE

Bank size, as a determinant of exploitation-path shape, shows a rather interesting difference in its effect on cost-reducing as against revenue-producing applications. The quantitative data presented in Chapter III clearly relates bank size to the exploitation of the cost-reducing capability. The larger the bank, the greater are the potential savings; hence the stronger is the incentive to exploit cost savings. A rather more complex relationship with respect to the revenue-producing capability is evident. The incentive to exploit this capability is strongest at the two extremes of the size scale—in the largest and the smallest of automated banks.

The smaller the bank adopting the new technology, the greater is the pressure to seek and exploit revenue-producing applications. Because of its relatively limited utilization of machine capacity and the comparatively small cost savings available to amortize the cost of the installation, the small bank is pressed hard to spread its computer costs over as wide a range of applications as possible.

Even small dollar amounts of additional revenues generated by the sale of relatively simple computer applications represent a larger percentage of total bank revenues in smaller banks. A revenue-producing application that a large bank might consider not worth the trouble will often be a highly desirable source of added income to a small bank, well worth the cost and effort needed to develop and market it.

The larger the bank and the assets at its disposal, the higher is the potential for additional income that can be generated by capable management of these assets. The additional ¼ per cent yield which, hopefully, may be gained by employing computer programs in its asset management will obviously show a higher rate of return on the investment in systems design and programming for the bank investing $100 million, rather than $10 million.

There is, however, a significant difference in these patterns of exploitation when their *level* is considered. The small bank will tend to seek additional revenues with level-II applications, which can be installed with relatively limited technical sophistication. Revenue production at level-III applications, on the other hand, requires a high order of skill and EDP sophistication. Only the larger banks are able to afford at the present the high-level specialization.

In going through hundreds of responses to the ABA survey questionnaire, the writer noticed the small number of banks that employed "operations research personnel." Most of these few had assets over a billion dollars. Even if this term is too strict for the type of specialist needed, the advantage of the large bank is made quite evident by these responses.

BANK LOCATION

The geographic location of any bank determines, to a great extent, the degree to which it can exploit the computer's revenue-producing capability at level II, particularly the upper ranges of this level. New services, particularly those not traditionally provided by banks, can be successfully merchandized only where there is demand for them. This demand originates with other firms who will benefit by computer exploitation but who do not operate installations of their own. Thus, the composition, density, and size of business firms in any bank's trading area determine the scope and range of revenue-producing services it may offer. An equally powerful constraint imposed by geographic location is the existence of competing data-processing facilities—usually service bureaus—who can offer a similar range of services.

An examination of several Booz, Allen & Hamilton evaluations of the feasibility of diversifying bank services shows a careful market survey of potential users in the immediate area. Typically, a satisfactory market was found to exist in locations where (1) a large number of small firms with relatively homogeneous needs tended to concentrate; or (2) a few medium-sized firms—not necessarily in the same industry—had a real need for EDP but were not large enough to justify computer operation.

In some instances the nature of the local demand may even encourage exploitation at level III. One bank, for example, undertook the processing of some highly sophisticated statistical analyses for a chemical manufacturer in its vicinity. Another performs structural design computations for an engineering client. In its pursuit of diversified revenue-producing services, one bank is aggressively attempting to minimize the constraint of location. It has been successful in selling some computer services on a statewide basis and to a few customers more than a thousand miles away.

5.4. A Relatively Unique Set of Determinants

Section 5.3 reviewed the determinants that help shape each firm's exploitation-path, starting with those common to the entire banking system and concluding with those that are highly specific for the individual bank. It should be noted that even industry-wide determinants may be felt in varying degrees by different firms. The institutional changes in checking-account practices, for example, put considerably heavier pressure on the "retail-oriented" banks than on their wholesaling competitors. Thus the combination of industry-wide and specific determinants confronts each individual bank with a relatively unique set of opportunities and constraints. No two banks face an identical set of determinants within which their exploitation-paths are to be traced.

The actual tracing of the path, as noted earlier, is accomplished by the decisions of each firm's management. Even highly rational decision-making depends on the perception of the environmental pressures and the available alternatives, the projection of the consequences of each possible alternative and, finally, the evaluation of such consequences in terms of the decision-making objectives or values.[13] Each of these elements may be perceived or evaluated differently by different firms' managements, depending on a set of highly individualized constraints. Such constraints are based in each firm's historical orientation, operating characteristics, goals and taboos, as well as its attitude to uncertainty and risk. Furthermore, a firm's "management" is, in the final analysis, a combination of individuals of varied backgrounds, intellectual disciplines, needs, capabilities, and values. One would therefore expect to find little unanimity in decisions reached by different managements, except in situations where (1) the environmental determinants are so overwhelmingly powerful and distinct as to be uniformly perceived by almost all observers; or (2) the principal variables are subject to quantification and measurement, with a reasonably high degree of certainty, against a clearly defined and universally accepted goal (for example, dollars against a profit-maximization goal).

In our case study in Chapter II, the spectacular increase in the volume and cost of paper-handling by banks since World War II represents a powerful set of determinants subject to little, if any, differences in perception or interpretation. This is a clear illustra-

---

13. For typical decision-making models, see: Newman and Sumner, *op. cit.,* Chapters 12–15; and I. D. J. Bross, *Design for Decision* (New York: The Macmillan Company, 1961).

tion of the first of the two conditions just stated. Similarly, cost-reducing applications—particularly at level-I capability—are easily evaluated in dollars and cents with a reasonable degree of confidence in forecasts or projections. They are representative of the second condition for unanimity in decision-making.

At the other end of the scale—far less likely to be uniformly perceived and evaluated—lie (1) the more subtle variables implicit in local competition, relationships with depositors and correspondents, and the demands of the local business community; and (2) the greater uncertainty associated with forecasting the potential success of new revenue-producing applications and the difficulty of quantifying such intangibles as "customer satisfaction" or "improved control."

This line of reasoning serves to explain the empirical findings noted earlier. Almost every bank adopting the new technology first exploited its purely cost-reducing capability in mechanizing routine paper work. Just as striking as the unanimity displayed in selecting the first set of applications is the almost complete lack of unanimity in the selection of the second, third, and subsequent sets of applications.

In the more abstract terms of the exploitation-path traced by each bank we find an almost universal low-level take off in the cost-reducing direction, represented by the almost-horizontal line in Figure 5.3. Beyond this initial phase, further application-selection decisions are made by individual managements who perceive what we have shown to be a unique set of determinants confronting each firm in the industry. It would, therefore, be pure coincidence (or an irrational game of follow-the-leader) if individual firms were to trace identical paths in their exploitation of the new technology. We should accordingly expect an almost unique exploitation-path for each firm adopting automation, particularly as the firm enlarges the repertoire of its applications.

Blindly following the leader has not been adopted as a popular strategy, as evidenced by the extremely diverse combinations of applications adopted by individual banks. The relatively high cost of "software" and training, the built-in delay in implementation, and the prevalent use of outside experts to evaluate and recommend new applications may explain the high degree of rationality in not blindly following the leader. A greater degree of indulgence in this dubious pastime may become evident in the future. The same factors of prepackaged programs, greater availability of technical skills, and so forth, which we noted in the comparison of early and recent computer installations (Chapter III), will undoubtedly make it easier for firms to jump into new applications without careful study of their own specific needs and opportunities. Although some services selected in this manner might prove worthwhile, others could well prove disastrous.

Even when we allow for a certain degree of follow-the-leader irrationality, we submit that a relatively unique exploitation-path will be charted by each individual firm adopting the new technology. It can be even more positively stated that there cannot be a normative or optimal exploitation-path for any industry or system taken as a whole. The number and shape of possible exploitation-paths that individual firms in an industry might follow is virtually infinite. In practice, one would expect to see several broad typologies of exploitation-path patterns develop. At this stage of relatively limited diversification, it is too early to attempt a typological classification of exploitation-paths. In the next chapter, however, brief case histories of four banks are presented to illustrate existing variations in patterns of exploitation.

VI

Contrasts in Automation— Four Case Experiences

Both the empirical evidence and the conceptual analysis, presented in the preceding chapters, point out the remarkable similarity in exploitation patterns evident in the early stages of automation and the growing diversity that follows. The empirical data, furthermore, show that the large majority of automated banks are still at the early—and therefore common—stage of their exploitation-path. For this reason it is perhaps somewhat premature to attempt a rigorous typological classification. Accordingly, this chapter should be regarded as only a tentative step in this direction.

Four banks were selected to illustrate what appear to be early indications of significant differences in automation patterns. The four banks range widely in size: two are among the largest in the system, one is medium-size, and one is among the smallest to attempt automation. It would have been desirable, particularly as a basis for subsequent discussion of the impacts of automation, to examine a bank that actively exploits level-III computer applications. Unfortunately no such sample was available at the time of writing in 1964. Two of the banks showed a limited degree of exploitation at this level—a mere scratching of the surface. To the best of the writer's knowledge, however, these banks are as advanced in this respect as any to be currently found.

As already pointed out in the Introduction, the names and locations assigned each bank are fictitious. All other relevant information that does not directly identify the banks is factual.

6.1. Essex County National Bank

This is a medium-sized bank, with close to a quarter of a billion dollars in deposits and twenty-six branches, all located within thirty miles of its head office in a New England city. This bank's automation program, under the leadership of its vice-president for operations has been directed almost exclusively to cost-saving applications, with the exception of the processing of a few customer payrolls. Excessive labor-turnover rates and the prospect of mounting volumes of paperwork were cited as the principal stimulants for the introduction of automation. Coupled with these was the desire to make better use of personnel in the smaller branch offices.

Essex County's experience is interesting primarily as an example of extensive and highly effective exploitation of automation's cost-reducing capability in the improvement of existing services. Revenue production is only slightly exploited in payroll processing, and even this service was available to bank customers before computerization. Therefore, there is no exploitation of level-II capability. On the other hand, in its pursuit of cost-reducing applications, Essex County is beginning to utilize some of the computer's level-III capability.

As has been typical of check-handling operations in most banks, the clerical staff consisted principally of women, supplemented by a changing stream of part-time workers. Because of its location, this bank often relied on part-time college students, particularly in its proof-and-transit department. Turnover rates were high; up to 50 per cent on the night shift. Today this department presents a very different picture. The majority of its employees are men, who work full-time and are paid on a straight

1 0 7

incentive system. The turnover rate among incentive workers has been virtually zero in the three years that the system has been in operation.

Each operator's output—in terms of "items handled"—is recorded daily. The average output over a two-week period determines the hourly pay rate for the following two weeks. Standard production rates for each type of work and each machine model are established for each hourly rate to be earned. Incentive hourly pay rates range from $1.50 to $2.80, as compared to $1.25 paid for similar nonincentive work. Each employee's earnings may fluctuate up or down, depending on the preceding two-weeks' output. Any errors that an operator makes or permits to go past him are detected in subsequent operations and result in standard penalties in computing his next earnings rate. Conversely, if any batch of work given to an operator contains excessive errors or other unusual difficulties, the operator is permitted to "sign off" his incentive time. He is then paid standard rates for the period so signed-off, and his average hourly output is not depressed by the problem batch.

The incentive system is a comparatively simple one, compared with many industrial applications. This is believed to be one of the few incentive systems in use in 1964 in any commercial bank. It is significant, however, that a 1963 bulletin of NABAC suggests an incentive system for consideration by its member banks.[1] Essex County National Bank, in conjunction with its incentive system, has generated a series of management reports that improve production scheduling and control by making available prompt and comprehensive information. Daily reports of output (by type of work and operator), errors in processing, machine running times for each type of work, number and percentage of items rejected by the sorter-reader, and so forth, supply much of the foundation of management-information systems. However the primary emphasis at this stage is centered on management control, rather than planning.

---

1. National Association of Bank Auditors and Controllers, *NABAC Research Institute Bulletin,* Vol. 4, No. 1 (July 11, 1963).

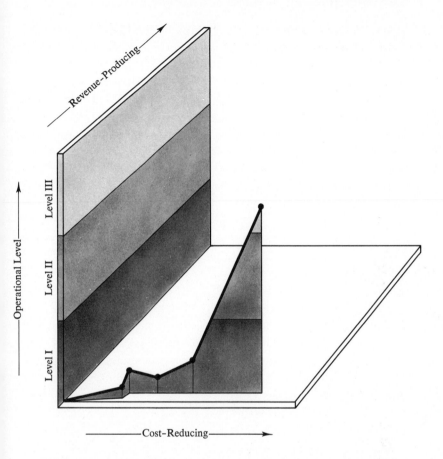

Figure 6.1—Exploitation Path: Essex County National Bank

The changes in its employee complement and compensation, as well as the control information generated by this bank's computer center, represent the beginnings of penetration into level-III capability. We would depict this bank's experience with automation and its current status by an exploitation-path of the form shown in Figure 6.1. This path shows substantial progress in the cost-reducing direction and only negligible penetration in the revenue-producing direction. Exploitation is confined to relatively low ranges of level I, followed by a small penetration into

109

level III. The computer's capability to generate new services (level II) is not exploited.[2]

With this pattern of exploitation, Essex County's experience already shows a number of interesting impacts. Most striking is the increased productivity achieved in incentive-based operations. Almost every knowledgeable operating officer was greatly surprised at and admired the hourly outputs. It is estimated that this bank's output per operator-hour is almost double the output considered normal by most automated banks. By the same token, the hourly rates earned (ranging from $2.10 to $2.80) are considered exceptionally high by most bankers but well worth the increase in productivity. Aside from the number of employees involved, the Essex County experience indicates some changes in the structure and orientation of bank employment.

Several writers have commented on the growing similarity between the office and the factory. Ida Hoos emphasizing this tendency, gives several factors as evidence. One is the measurability, by objective count, of clerical outputs, being undertaken by economy- and production-minded managements. Other similarities she points out are the presence of mechanical equipment, high noise levels, and the use of shift work. "Thus, the machine operator in the modern office works under conditions similar to those of her blue-smocked sister in the plant."[3]

The factory-like appearance of bank operations is much more apparent in the largest banks we visited than in Essex County. Rows upon rows of clattering machines each tended by its operator, messengers wheeling in batches of "raw material," distributing it to work stations, and then removing the finished product to other departments. These are the impressions of a large city bank's proof-and-transit department. They are, however, little different from the same department's appearance in preautomation days. Nor is the three-shift operation peculiar to the com-

---

2. Note that although the Exploitation Path must, of necessity, go *through* level II in the diagram, there are no round dots on it at this level, indicating that no level-II applications are being exploited.

3. Hoos, *op. cit.*, p. 124.

puter age. In the case of Essex County and its big city counter-parts, the "paper factory" flavor of automation is evident more in the way in which the department is managed and directed.

In the visit to Essex County and in conversations with its supervisors, the writer was struck forcibly by the many similari-ties to his experiences as a consultant in industrial plants: the supervisor's desk covered with production reports, his concern for the night shift's record, the lower output posted by Jones yesterday, and the best way to distribute the afternoon's work load through the department. These are the true indicators of the degree to which clerical work is becoming factory-like. When one adds to these the supervisor's direct concern with production costs in his department and the problems of routing work so as to balance loads on two computer systems and meet tight dead-lines, then the parallels between a clerical supervisor and an industrial foreman are almost complete. This represents a big step toward the "professionalization" of supervisory work.

The advent of the "paper factory" will presumably lead to increased task specialization in clerical work, quite probably accompanied by many of the now-familiar problems of the blue-collar worker. This is in the realm of speculation. It is evident however that the extension of the exploitation-path in the cost-reducing dimension at increasingly higher levels of exploitation will probably result in structural changes that will accelerate the advent of the "paper factory." Most bankers shudder when asked whether this trend may bring about unionization of banks' cleri-cal employees. Several believe there is a distinct possibility of this.

Essex County's experience is also interesting in terms of the backgrounds of its supervisors and managers. This bank filled all supervisory jobs by promotion from within. A few attempts to bring in nonbankers from outside the organization did not prove successful. It was far more effective to teach computer technology to bankers than to attempt to teach banking to EDP specialists. This experience applied to the supervisory and junior-officer levels. No additions or changes were made in senior-officer positions. The vice-president in charge of operations—the sparkplug of the entire automation program—is a comparatively young man in his early forties of somewhat unusual background. His education, before joining the bank, consisted of an undergraduate mathematics degree at Massachusetts Institute of Technology and a master's in business administration at Dartmouth. He was given a relatively free hand in planning and implementing the bank's automation program. Top management accepted his recommendations without a detailed understanding of computer systems and their implications.

In 1964 this bank made its first change in formal organizational structure. Its vice-president for operations was transferred to a new assignment. Instead of continuing to run the routine operations he had set up, he was placed in charge of planning and developing new systems and applications. The change was made at the vice-president's own request. In his new function, this officer plans to develop management-information systems and broaden the scope of computer applications beyond the exclusive needs of the operating department. He also believes that some attention should be given to the development of new services at this stage. Because of the size of the bank, the new function will involve only a few key people. One of its most important tasks, according to its new head, will be educational. It will attempt to persuade top management to use the computer's decision-making, level-III capabilities, in contrast to the "seat of the pants" approach to business management.

One final observation on Essex County's experience is appropriate. This bank has traditionally believed in decentralization. Its branch managers were, and are, expected to assume all responsibility for their own customer relations. With the introduction of the computer, all check-processing and statement-mailings were centralized in a newly acquired operations building. The intent was merely to transfer a certain amount of clerical work but not to alter the responsibility or authority of branch managers. When branch managers showed some tendency to blame statement errors on "that computer setup downtown," the bank

1 1 2

modified its procedures. At the time of writing in 1964, the mailing operations were being transferred back to each branch office. This move was designed to encourage branch managers to assume full responsibility. It is also believed that some cost savings will be realized. Branch personnel would be able to attend to statement-mailing in their spare time. Full-time operations clerks formerly assigned this task will be freed for other work. As far as this bank is concerned automation has not, and need not, result in centralization of authority and responsibility. The bank officers are prepared to modify its processing systems to achieve the organizational balance considered most desirable.

6.2. Manufacturers National Bank

Most experts would rate this bank with total assets of $50 million as too small to warrant a computer installation. Despite expert ratings, the Manufacturers National Bank has been operating a computer for some three years. Considerable determination and ingenuity was needed to make this possible. Extreme frugality was called for in the selection of hardware, coupled with a determined and aggressive approach to its exploitation.

This bank's system is built around two G-15 computers (originally manufactured by Bendix Electronics, which was absorbed by Control Data Corporation). The G-15, a first-generation, vacuum-tube unit is considered technologically obsolete. Its comparatively low speed, however, is partially compensated for by its flexibility. This unit has been adapted to accept a variety of inputs: MICR-coding, punched cards, magnetic tape, and paper tape. It is also comparatively inexpensive to own or lease.

Most interesting, from our point of view, is the way this equipment has been put to work. Aside from converting the bank's own demand-deposit accounting, the main effort has been directed at the development of new customer services. Some forty clients have been serviced with a wide variety of computer applications, many of them entirely divorced from traditional banking services. This bank's exploitation-path is of the form illustrated in Figure 6.2. It will be seen that following the customary take

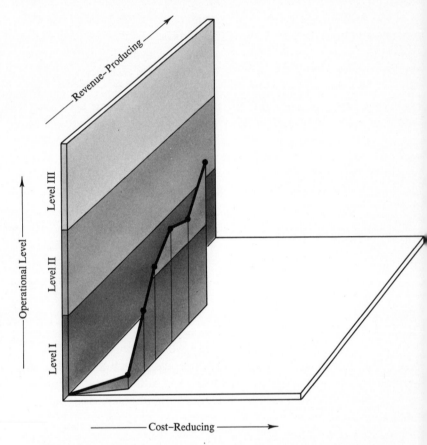

Figure 6.2—Exploitation Path: Manufacturers National Bank

off in the cost-reducing, level-I direction, the path veers inward and upward. Revenue production, at increasingly higher stages of level II, is the principal characteristic of Manufacturers National's exploitation-path. This level-II orientation is reflected in the organizational structure adopted, the key personnel involved, the services offered by the bank, and the attitude of its top management.

The computer installation is operated by a separate and relatively independent division of the bank, the Automated Services Center of New England. All letterheads, advertising, and promotional literature feature the name "Automated Services Center of New England," subtitled (in small print) "a division of Manufacturers National Bank." The Center enjoys almost complete autonomy and is treated as an independent "profit center." It sells its services to a variety of clients, one of which is the bank itself. Services supplied to the various bank divisions are billed at rates designed to yield a profit to the Center. At this stage the concept is perhaps more significant than the actual service rates charged, since these are primarily internal "transfer prices." The important consideration is that the Center's officers are expected to be completely responsible for its own operation and profit. Officials even stated that outside work was given preference over the bank's own accounting needs. The Center is, significantly enough, an associate member of the Association of Data Processing Service Organizations.

Of the Center's nine officers, seven have nonbanking backgrounds. Their previous experience ranges from merchandising to EDP and professional engineering. The vice-president in charge of the Center is an experienced computer-systems engineer; its manager is a merchandiser with no previous banking experience. Other specialists include a programmer, a registered professional engineer, and a systems engineer. Only two supervisors, primarily concerned with demand-deposit accounting, are long-time bank employees.

The variety of services that the Center offers is listed in its promotional literature: general ledger accounting, cost distributions, payroll, inventory control and statistical forecasting, sales analysis, educational statistical summaries, managerial-control reports, multiple-listing service, engineering calculations, property assessment, and tax collection. The Center's manager actively seeks out clients and applications whether new or repeats.

The bank's president, although retaining a veto over services to be offered, permits and encourages an extremely broad spectrum of clients and services. The Center advertises its services, emphasizing their broad range and flexibility.

An indication of the variety of customers serviced is this partial list, featured in one of the Center's advertisements: a well-known restaurant chain, the local public school system, a nationally famous industrial manufacturer, the YMCA, local real estate board, a neighboring bank, the local city administration, a charitable federation, a newspaper, a telephone-answering service, and a hospital. Some of the Center's clients are surprisingly remote geographically: a telephone company in California and a real-estate listing service in Indiana. Some clients are local plants of large, national corporations; others are small local businesses.

The operating philosophy behind the Manufacturers National Bank's approach to automation was featured in an editorial in a financial periodical and was confirmed in an interview with the bank's president. It is basically grounded in the following beliefs.

1. Banks of necessity have become expert in handling masses of paper work. Technological improvements have continually introduced better equipment for this purpose. In all but the largest banks, such equipment lies idle a substantial part of the time. With the advent of high-cost computers, medium-size and small banks cannot afford idle time. Ways must be found to make full use of the new equipment and the paper-handling know-how possessed by the banking system.

2. If small, country banks are to retain their independence, they must generate earnings from nonbank operations. In this way they can afford to retain competent managers and avoid the threat of merger or domination by larger banks.

3. In a changing world costly experimentation is all too easily left to large banks. The service-bureau approach permits a small bank to exploit technological change in improving its own operations and their effectiveness. The president pointed out that some experimentation can be done only in big banks, but there is a great deal of experimentation that smaller banks not only can

but should perform. He stated that one of the responsibilities of the directors of a bank is to assure a steady flow of ideas to be tried.

4. Finally, a bank's principal function should be viewed on a broader basis than the sale of money. Because banks have always dealt with symbols and information, their competence in this area should be broadened. In this view a bank has only one broad commodity to sell—service to the community.

The road to automation taken by the Manufacturers National Bank has not been an easy one. The merchandising and selling of services has proved a challenging task. Competition from independent service bureaus and those of equipment manufacturers has been keen. The Automated Service Center only began to break even after three years of operation. Its initiation and survival is in no small measure due to the perceptive and forward-looking qualities of the bank's president. Its present plans are focused on enlarging the market for new customer services, with greater emphasis on more sophisticated applications for its clients. Through engineering computations and other operations-research applications, it is seeking to penetrate into level III—revenue-producing services.

6.3. Metropolitan Bank and Trust Company

The Metropolitan Bank is one of the largest banks in the United States. It boasts total assets of several billion dollars and operates over one hundred branches. This bank's automation program was directed by its advanced-systems planning division and has gone through several stages of equipment additions and expansions. At present, computer applications are centered on the improvement of existing, high-volume operations. Substantial cost-savings are claimed for the new systems, particularly when allowance is made for the growth in volume of operations since the conversion. In addition to the primary cost reductions, the bank has obtained significant additions to revenue as a by-product of these applications. From the bank's point of view, however, one of the most important results has been the increased centralization made possible by the computer.

In contrast with Essex County National Bank's experience, Metropolitan Bank discovered that its operating department could not cope effectively with automation planning. In 1958 the advanced-systems planning division was set up to explore the potentials of computer and electronic-data processing. All officers of the new division were hired from the outside, several of them from a well-known consulting firm. Their previous experience, almost exclusively nonbanking, included scientific, academic, computer technology, and consulting, and this orientation of the division's staff has persisted. Only two junior officers, in a total staff of eighty, represent promotions from within the bank.

Realizing that a common machine language was still several years off, two purely internal computer applications were designed and installed. Employee payroll and benefit programs were automated, primarily as a training ground for technicians and personnel. By early 1959 planning was initiated on demand-deposit accounting. This was seen as the area of greatest potential savings. The division made a comprehensive study of current and anticipated costs. Conversion of demand-deposit accounting was started in March 1961 and completed in April 1963. Some indication of the magnitude of the task is the fact that more than half a million accounts were involved and an average of more than one and a half million checks had to be handled daily.

The large volumes of work to be processed made substantial savings possible. Bank officers estimated that, without automation, an additional eight hundred employees would be needed to handle current check volumes. The transition was achieved without any layoffs. Normal attrition and turnover, in fact, were so high as to make some new hirings necessary even during the conversion period. It was estimated that by September 1963, approximately two and a half years after conversion had begun, savings had repaid the full cost of planning and installation.

To achieve these savings Metropolitan Bank went at least part of the way taken by Essex County. Although it did not establish an incentive pay system, Metropolitan prepares weekly reports showing actual employee output as compared to a budgeted standard. These reports, which cover some 8,500 clerical jobs of a repetitive nature, are sent to department managers and supervisors. The same reports are used for establishing standard costs for the repetitive operations.

The bank's demand-deposit system also yields a number of revenue-producing by-products. It is estimated that an additional $360,000 per year is collected by the bank in the form of service charges. These were either missed or overlooked by the account-analysis procedures in effect before the computer installation. Another by-product of the computerized demand-deposit accounting is a profitability-analysis report on each account. The computer distinguishes between collected and uncollected funds. This permits the bank to compute the average gross balance and average collected balance for each account. Thus the bank can spot any "kiting" by depositors—whether intentional or not. In addition, each branch manager can readily see the revenue yield from each account and compare it to the cost of services rendered. Any account showing a loss of more than twenty-five dollars a month or a continual loss (of any amount) for six consecutive months is "flagged" and reported to the branch manager's superior.

The profitability-analysis reports are but one step in the tightened supervision over branch operations. In contrast with Essex County's intent to continue or even increase decentralization, Metropolitan has deliberately used its computer installation to increase centralization. One of the primary objectives of automation in this bank is to bring about greater uniformity and more stringent control over its wide branch operations. The bank's history of mergers and consolidations was evident in a diversity of branch methods and attitudes, which top management considered excessive. In particular, the merger of two major bank systems with markedly different characteristics resulted in undesirable heterogeneity of branch operations. The computer made it possible to introduce uniform check-processing methods, cost accounting, and branch supervision standards.

The same intent to increase centralization is evident in a major revision in the bank's organizational structure made in 1963. A unified bank operations group was consolidated under an executive vice-president to service all bank departments and divisions. Before this change each division (for example, trust, international, U.S.) had its own operations department to minister to its own administrative needs. The consolidated bank operations division is in charge of all computer operations, regardless of application or division for which the work is processed. Metropolitan, to the best of our knowledge, is the first major bank to consolidate bank-wide operations in this type of formal structure. In addition to increased centralization, bank officers feel that the new grouping, now given representation at the top of the hierarchical structure, has raised the stature of operations and its personnel. It is seen as a distinct move to "professionalize" the status of operations managers and administrators.

While the new bank operations group is responsible for all computer processing operations, it is not charged with the planning and design of new systems. This is a task divided among three staff departments, all of which report to a different executive vice-president and thus belong to a separate division. Most immediately concerned with designing computer applications is the advanced-systems planning division discussed earlier. This unit studies the feasibility of new applications, designs and programs them, and then trains personnel in their operation. Once "debugged," the new application is turned over to the bank operations group for routine processing. A corporate planning unit and an organization planning unit, both staff departments, are also involved with planning connected with the computer systems. The former is concerned with such items as asset management and improved budgeting; the latter, with the organizational and communication line changes resulting from systems improvements. Both these departments rely on advanced-systems planning to prepare detailed systems analyses and computer programs in implementing any changes or applications. All three staff departments report to the executive vice-president for corporate plans and staff. It may be noted in passing that at a neighboring city bank, of comparable size, the equivalent department (named automation planning) is part of the operations division. It reports to the executive vice-president for operations rather than to a separate staff division or group.

It is also interesting to note Metropolitan Bank's approach to automated customer services, as contrasted with that at Manufacturers National. Within advanced-systems planning there is a new-customer services unit, which operates, in effect, a service bureau for outside customers. The selection and approval of new services is rather tightly controlled, however. Before any application is installed it must be approved by the pricing committee, a high-level committee consisting of the heads of the trust, national banking, planning, and operations departments. They establish the pricing policy for each service offered. In 1964 only three external services were offered, all of which were available to customers even before the computer's advent. Of these, only account reconciliation was in wide use (over 200 customers). The other two—payroll processing and correspondent-bank accounting—were in the early stages of market development. Current policy, formed within the constraints of the pricing committee, is to limit future customer services to traditional banking functions. Bank officers see little point in going into competition with commercial service bureaus offering a wide range of automated services.

Metropolitan's approach to the sale of customer services is also strikingly different from Manufacturers National. Instead of the direct selling undertaken by officers of the computer center, Metropolitan Bank markets its services through branch managers and officers. When a service is adopted and proved, branch personnel are instructed in its marketing. They are supplied with kits and information to cope with commonly asked questions. When a potential customer's interest reaches the point where

121

technical details need to be ironed out, service bureau personnel are brought in. The difference in approach between Metropolitan and Manufacturers National is, of course, a reflection of their significantly different attitude to automated customer services. This difference in attitude can be traced back to the tremendous size disparity between the two banks. The tendency of the large bank to seek additions to revenue by improving internal management and operations, in contrast to the small bank's search for new customer services, was discussed and explained in the preceding chapter.

In conceptual terms, Metropolitan's exploitation-path takes the shape illustrated in Figure 6.3. The path is characterized by extensive exploitation of level-I capability, at successively higher stages. This level of exploitation is prominent in the pursuit of both cost-reducing and revenue-producing applications. The trend towards the former is more pronounced than the latter, but orientation is not as determinedly cost-reducing as was the path traced by Essex County National Bank. Although absolute cost-savings are considerably higher in Metropolitan's case—due to its larger volume of activity—it has not exploited this capability to the same relative extent as Essex County has. Incentive pay is not used to compensate operators, nor are operator-output reports used to schedule, control, or motivate departmental production. Therefore, there is no penetration of level-III capability at this stage.

In the pursuit of the revenue-producing capability, Metropolitan's exploitation-path shows a significant difference from that traced by Manufacturers National. The latter's revenues were generated primarily through new and nontraditional customer services (upper ranges of level II). By contrast, Metropolitan's exploitation-path does not penetrate level II at all. The bulk of its revenue production is achieved by improved controls over billing for services rendered and changes in reporting procedures that focus branch managers' attention to account profitability. These are achieved by relatively sophisticated exploitation of level-I capability. A minor contribution to revenue production is

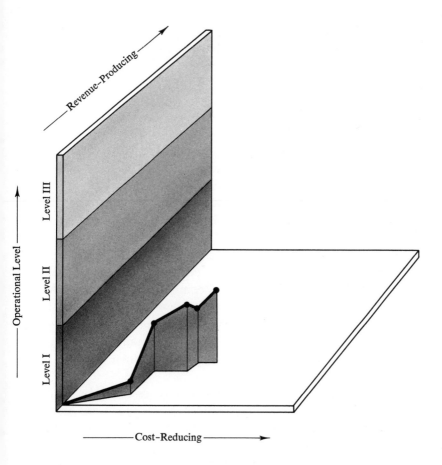

Figure 6.3—Exploitation Path: Metropolitan Bank and Trust Company

also made by the three customer services currently being offered. As these are automated services formerly offered by other means, they too are properly classed in level I.

Despite a highly technically skilled staff, Metropolitan's officers have not assigned high priority to the development of unusually sophisticated operations-research techniques. They feel that the large volumes of routine clerical work justify additional concentration in level-I systems design. This immediate demand

123

on technical and human resources leaves comparatively little time for research into model-making or simulation.

6.4. Fidelity Bank and Trust Company

This is another of the country's largest banks, with several billion dollars in assets and deposits. This bank's automation program was reviewed earlier, in Chapter III.

Fidelity's exploitation of automation was guided and planned by a staff department—methods research—somewhat similar to the Metropolitan arrangement. There are, however, a number of significant differences. First, Fidelity's methods research department existed even before computer processing was first considered, and it initiated all computer planning. In Metropolitan, by contrast, the operations department initiated the investigation and was later replaced by a newly hired staff group. Comparatively few additions to Fidelity's staff personnel were needed to undertake new systems planning when computer feasibility was first studied.

A second significant difference is represented by Fidelity's policy of "spinning off" new applications, as they were debugged. This practice consists of transferring a nucleus of trained personnel from methods research to the appropriate operating department when each application is installed. The resultant turnover in methods research personnel, according to bank officers, was more than made up for in smooth conversion and continued close liaison between methods research and the operating departments. This procedure is also viewed as a sound educational device because it spreads systems-conscious personnel throughout the organization.

In terms of personnel backgrounds, Fidelity's methods research is staffed by approximately equal numbers of bankers and nonbankers. Among the nonbankers there is a wide variety of backgrounds and experiences. The department is headed by a vice-president—a banker by training—with an extremely broad range of interests and a forward-looking orientation.

Computer systems have not increased centralization at Fidelity. Within its banking departments, branch operations were not significantly affected even when accounting and check-handling functions were centralized for computer processing. Similarly, no attempt was made to consolidate all computer operations into a single center. Separate, and relatively autonomous, operations divisions, each with its own computer installation, service the banking and trust departments. Fidelity officers believe that this autonomy in operations provides a more flexible and responsive service to each department. As automation technology becomes more sophisticated it becomes increasingly difficult for the layman to evaluate the automated department's performance. In this sense, the men in top management are laymen, called upon to judge highly technical operations. (This is the major problem posed by Victor Thompson, who sees a gap developing between the manager's "ability" and his "power."[4]) At Fidelity at least one solution to this problem has been attempted. By maintaining two autonomous and, in a sense, competitive automated departments, the management can compare the arguments and performance of two sets of experts. This arrangement is considered preferable to an audit or critique by an outside consultant, as both departments function within the same organizational environment and within the same goal and value structure.

Fidelity has installed over half a dozen routine internal applications, primarily cost-reducing in nature. It also runs periodic, special-purpose programs designed by methods research, which are also primarily cost-reducing in nature. They are designed to substitute a few minutes of machine time for many hours of manual work to produce the same analytical results. These applications are typical of Fidelity's approach to cost reduction. The general orientation seems to focus on ingenious programming of

---

4. Victor Thompson, *Modern Organization* (New York: Alfred Knopf, 1961).

a variety of operations, rather than an all-out drive to raise and control productivity in high-volume, repetitive clerical work.

Automated, revenue-producing customer services, at this stage, are limited to payroll processing and account reconciliation. Both were available to Fidelity customers before computerization and therefore do not represent new services made possible by the computer. On the other hand, a revolving-credit consumer-loan program was recently installed by Fidelity only because it could be processed with a computer. It represents a new revenue-producing, although fairly traditional, banking service made possible by automation. Like Metropolitan, but in contrast to Manufacturers National, Fidelity does not intend to expand its repertory of new customer services into nontraditional banking services. Although it does not have the same formal constraint, in the form of a pricing committee, Fidelity believes that concentration on internal applications will prove more rewarding. Its reasoning is based on two premises. First, customer services exploiting the computer's level-II capability can be more effectively and cheaply sold by professional data-processing service bureaus. Second, more sophisticated services, at level-III exploitation, would entail disclosure of advanced techniques or ideas. It is felt that these will prove more rewarding if they are not publicized but are applied in the bank's own interests. Quite obviously, this attitude implies a high degree of confidence in Fidelity's ability to pioneer and develop significant innovations in the exploitation of the new technology.

This search for innovation is perhaps the most striking characteristic of Fidelity's exploitation of automation. Its methods research department is permitted considerable latitude in investigation and planning. The department's staff attempts to devote full attention to research for future applications, rather than tinker with modifications of present systems. To make this possible, separate methods units have been established in the banking and trust departments. These units attend to program modifications in their respective departments, relieving methods research from current operation planning. It is significant to note that some methods research personnel are studying techniques that they believe will not materialize as banking applications for some ten years. Others are studying hardware and "software" developments without any clear idea of where they would fit into banking operations at this point.

Considerable research has already gone into developing models and programs for portfolio and asset management, as well as computation of underwriting bids. For obvious reasons the bank is reluctant to discuss this work in any detail. It is believed that considerable progress has been made in the direction of revenue-producing exploitation through sophisticated computer utilization. Fidelity Bank's exploitation-path is illustrated by Figure 6.4.

We can see that the cost-reducing capability is pursued via a series of applications at varying ranges of level I. Cost reduction is exploited to a somewhat lesser degree than at Metropolitan but to a substantially greater extent than at Manufacturers National. Revenue production is exploited, to some extent, in three different ways. (1) Two traditional and formerly available customer services are automated; hence we find exploitation at level I, comparable to Metropolitan's. (2) A new, but rather traditional, service is offered—exploitation at the lower ranges of level II; this is comparable to early efforts of Manufacturers National. (3) Improved asset management through decision-making models and operations-research simulation techniques is being attempted. In the absence of any publishable data on the subject, it is presumed that these applications are either in the late stages of development or in the early stages of use. The penetration of the exploitation-path into the lower ranges of level III—representing these applications—is shown in dotted lines in Figure 6.4. Extensive and continual use of such programs will undoubtedly affect the decision-making process at Fidelity and will probably be reflected in adjustments in the organizational structure. To date no striking changes are evident.

It is interesting to note here that there appears to be a growing reluctance to discuss new computer developments. Several bank

127

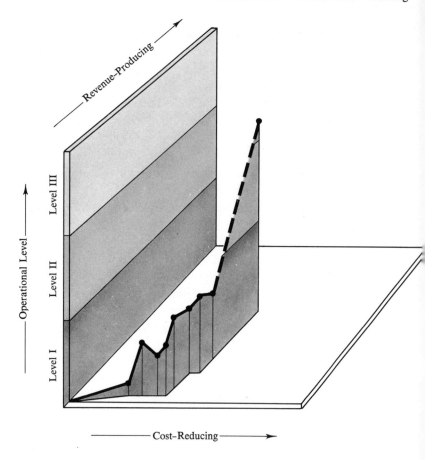

Figure 6.4—Exploitation Path: Fidelity Bank and Trust Company

officers remarked to the writer that the interchange of information between computer users has been restricted. Complete and total disclosure, which characterized the early automation stages in banking, is apparently no longer the case. Nor are the "packaged" and widely available programs publicized by equipment manufacturers regarded as the latest state of the art. As one banker put it, "The manufacturers' systems are useful only for the laggards, not the leaders."

If this observation is valid, then the effectiveness of the manufacturers' contribution towards higher-level exploitation, noted in the preceding chapter, is limited. Although equipment manufacturers undoubtedly command top-level expertise in computer technology, they possess only secondhand knowledge of any user's problems, attitudes, and experience. For this reason, highly sophisticated computer applications may have to be developed by the banks' own personnel—at considerable research cost and effort. The apparent trend toward greater secrecy is thus quite understandable and may be expected to grow. A new element would then be added to interbank competition—a kind of "secret process," which is commonly associated with manufacturing rather than service industries. In view of the skill and investment prerequisites inherent in innovations of this type, the comparative advantage of the large bank would appear even more pronounced. Such advantage could also prove long-lived, because no tangible product would appear on the market for competitors to examine, analyze, copy. There are implications for the scholar too. Future researchers may find increasing difficulty in determining the specific applications to which computer technology is put —particularly the most advanced ones. A conceptual framework, such as the one attempted here, may however prove useful in interpreting the direction and level of exploitation through its observed impacts.

VII

The Impacts of Automation–
Empirical and Theoretical

Few topics, in either popular or scholarly literature, have received as much recent attention as the impacts of automation. Quite understandably, the most comprehensive studies and controversies focused on the impacts of automation on employment, though Congressional committees and numerous conferences have spent countless days in attempting to forecast the impacts of automation on our economy as a whole.[1]

An astute and highly informed observer, James R. Bright, concludes that:

> ... In the face of ... different industrial environments and the variety of automation effects, plus the influence of other factors at work in some cases, only one conclusion is possible: *The net impact of automation on a plant or even an industry cannot be derived reliably from a generality. No one kind of experience—even an increase of the maintenance force —is a certainty.*[2]

This chapter will probe the validity of Bright's conclusion as applied to bank automation. From this tight base a number of

---

1. Cf., U.S. Congress, House, Committee on Education and Labor, Subcommittee on Unemployment and the Impact of Automation, *Impact of Automation on Employment,* 87th Cong., June 1961. U.S. Congress, House, Joint Economic Committee, Subcommittee on Economic Stabilization, *Automation and Technological Change,* 84th Cong., October 1955.

2. Bright, *Automation and Management,* p. 194. Italics by Bright.

questions will be examined. What impacts of bank automation are evident? How meaningful can any discussion of the impacts of automation be? Can one firm's experience be another firm's guide? Finally, how valid are industry-wide or nationwide generalizations drawn from empirical case studies?

We will begin by stating quite frankly that our study of bank automation fails to reveal any radical impact as of the time of writing in 1964. We make this statement despite the fact that many banks already employ several high-powered computers and in the face of much talk of revolutionary change. This statement is justified not only by the writer's extensive interviews with bank officers but also by the questioning of consultants, technicians, and other experts in the field. It is confirmed by management consultants and technical experts active in the field of bank automation. Many of them feel that banking is on the "threshold of revolution" or "at the crossroads." None could point to any truly radical departures. Equally significant is the wide divergence of views as to the probable direction the anticipated revolution will take and its most likely impacts.

This chapter will examine impacts in four areas of general interest: employment, organizational structure, managerial responsibilities, and the firm's functions.

7.1. Impacts on Employment

The most evident impact of bank automation has undoubtedly been in the area of employment. Fewer clerical workers are able to cope with the volume of paper work, or alternately, sizable increases in volume of processing have been absorbed without proportionate increases in staff. Even this, however, is not evident in truly revolutionary proportions. Its full force has undoubtedly been masked by two important factors. First, the steadily growing volume of work processed by the banking system (Table 2.3, Chapter II) has offset the increase in operator productivity. Second, almost every automating bank has adopted a no-layoff policy. A Congressional committee report of June 1961, states: "Automation has apparently proceeded slowly enough so far to allow normal turnover to disguise some of its effects."[3] It will be recalled that high turnover rates characterized virtually all the operations converted to computer processing. Lower employment levels were thus achieved by a freeze on new hirings. In a sense, *future* job openings are being curtailed. Walker Buckingham refers to the same phenomenon:

> . . . the problem becomes not the worker who is fired but the worker who is not hired. The unions call this silent firing.[4]

Ida Hoos, in her study of office automation, also points to the ameliorating effects of an expanding economy and high turnover rates in the displaced jobs. She concludes:

> The persons most likely to be affected may be those not yet in the labor force, because machines are designed to handle an increasing volume of routine work more efficiently without a corresponding growth in the number of clerks required. The net effect is a reduction in clerical job opportunities for the younger sisters of the girls employed at present.[5] Automation's real problem children are those excluded by it rather than those involved in it.[6]

As far as the banking system specifically is concerned, two sources of quantitative evidence may be examined: the Booz, Allen & Hamilton client sample and a broader study by the U.S. Department of Labor. From the data presented in Tables 3.4 and 3.5 in Chapter III, reductions in personnel, as a per cent of the original number of employees, can be computed. Only three banks indicate reductions of less than 30 per cent; five

---

3. U.S. Congress, *Impact of Automation on Employment,* p. 13.

4. Walker Buckingham, *Automation, Its Impact on Business and People* (New York: Harper and Brothers, 1961), p. 119.

5. Based on the experience of Essex County National Bank, we are tempted to add that it may well be the *brothers,* rather than the sisters, who will be affected.

6. Hoos, *op. cit.,* p. 33.

banks show reductions of over 50 per cent. The average for all fifteen banks, for which these figures are available, indicates a reduction of 42.5 per cent in affected personnel. Table 3.6 indicates that for ten cooperative member banks, the average reduction is an even higher 59 per cent. As conversion normally takes at least two years, and as the labor turnover rate in the affected departments typically runs from 30 per cent to 50 per cent, it is apparent that the initial reduction in personnel can be readily accomplished through normal turnover and attrition.

Our computations from the sample data available tie in closely with the broader Labor Department study of September 1962.[7] The study estimates a reduction in employment in demand-deposit accounting and closely related activities at about 50 per cent (compared to the 42.5 per cent computed above). It also estimates that the new systems will create new jobs, equal to approximately one half of those eliminated. The study forecasts that by 1975 there will be a net reduction of some 22 per cent in job openings in banks as a result of automation. The projected growth in employment in insured commercial banks is expected to rise from 610,000 in 1960 to one million in 1975. Had there been no adoption of automation, employment would have reached 1,225,000 in 1975. Thus 225,000 *future* job opportunities will have been eliminated in a decade and a half. If any further evidence is needed to point up the longer-term impact of automation on employment, another figure from the Booz, Allen & Hamilton data can be cited. In Chapter III we noted that, for the twenty sample banks, the average cost-savings for the fifth year after installation are more than double (112 per cent) the immediate savings indicated. Furthermore, this impressive rise in savings is predicted in the face of an assumed 3 per cent annual increase in salary levels and in bank operations.

A significant difference should be noted in the basic premises underlying these two employment forecasts. The Booz, Allen & Hamilton data indicate the potential reduction in personnel em-

7. Rose Wiener, "Changing Manpower Requirements in Banking," *Monthly Labor Review* (September 1962), pp. 989–995.

ployed in the functions automated by the first one or two applications evaluated in the feasibility study. The Labor Department forecasts, by contrast, attempt to consider a broader view of bank automation—one in which new applications will create new jobs as well as eliminate old ones. The significant difference in the two views is readily related to the conceptual view of automation presented earlier. It is a difference based on the emphasis given to each dimension of capability of the new technology.

Reductions in employment result, for all practical purposes, from the exploitation of the cost-reducing capability. The further any bank's exploitation-path moves along the cost-reducing axis, the greater will the impact be in terms of reduced employment. The principal operating costs, in almost all service industries, are wages and salaries. Cost reductions, therefore, must inevitably lead to fewer personnel—either immediate or longerterm. This is the basis of the economic justification of the computer noted in Chapter III. Level-I exploitation, particularly at the lower, "mechanization" end of the scale, almost by definition relies on the substitution of mechanical devices for clerical operators.

The case experience of Essex County suggests that when costreducing can be exploited at level III, even more spectacular personnel reductions are possible. Exploiting the computer capability to plan, schedule, and control work flows, and superimposing a new reward structure, makes it possible to extend the exploitation-path even further along the cost-reducing axis. This raises an important question about the reliability of future employment forecasts in automated banks. The Labor Department study, for example, was based on the rates of productivity posted by a broad sample of automated banks. These represented exploitation of the cost-reducing capability at level I. Essex County, with only minimal penetration of level III, achieved productivity rates that most bankers estimated at almost double the average for the industry. If, in the future, most banks raise their costreduction exploitation to level III, an impressive increase in the average productivity rate should be reasonably anticipated. In this case, would not the current forecasts of the impact of automation on employment prove substantially understated?

An offsetting factor to personnel reduction, recognized in the Department of Labor study, is inherent in automation's revenue-producing capability. The exploitation of this capability need not result in any reduction in employment and, typically, would even tend to increase it. As the revenue-producing capability is exploited, additional work must be processed. It may involve the creation of entirely new functions or merely call for greater volumes of operations already performed by the bank. The difference is closely related to the level at which revenue production is exploited. The higher the level of exploitation, the more likely the creation of new functions and new jobs. At the upper ranges of level II—services far removed from traditional banking functions—banks will present employment opportunities in a variety of new specialties and job classifications.

Increased employment opportunities in banking will, therefore, depend on the extent to which the revenue-producing capability of automation is exploited, as well as the level of such exploitation. Forecasting the potential for new jobs in banking must assume some average, or typical, shape for banks' exploitation-paths. Is the path traced by Manufacturers National more typical than Essex County's, or Metropolitan's? A closely related question is the significance of these forecasts for the outlook in national employment. Will the new bank jobs created by aggressive, level-II exploitation represent a net addition to total employment, or will they reflect a displacement of jobs formerly performed in other industries or segments of the economy? Active supporters of the proposed Multer Bill, referred to in Chapter IV, apparently believe the second development is the more likely.

It is hardly surprising that there has been little unanimity among competent observers as to the impact of automation on employment. The significant variable appears to be the relative weight each analyst places on the different dimensions of automation's capability and the exploitation-path implicitly assumed.

Severe unemployment is forecast by those who focus their analysis on the cost-reducing capability almost exclusively, whereas increased employment is predicted by those who see revenue production as automation's principal capability.

The impact of automation on the *quality,* rather than the quantity, of employment, is no less controversial. At one extreme is the view that the computer takes over the monotonous, repetitive elements of clerical work, permitting employees to devote more of their working time to the challenging and creative phases of their jobs. Automation, in this view, results in an upgrading of jobs and employees. At the other extreme, automation is seen as a force downgrading jobs by routinizing, simplifying, and reducing skill levels of employees. Here again, the differences in opinion can be traced to differing perceptions of computer exploitation and the employees affected.

Level-III applications may well reduce the routine elements of a middle-manager's tasks and thereby upgrade his job. Level-I applications, on the other hand, result in little upgrading of the clerical jobs directly affected. Demand-deposit accounting, for example, admittedly eliminates the highly repetitive bookkeeping operation. The jobs of preparing the inputs and checking the outputs of the new system, however, can hardly be described as intellectually stimulating or highly creative. All too often the increased specialization generally accompanying office automation tends to increase the monotony of clerical jobs. A repetitive task that formerly constituted a part-time element of several jobs is often consolidated into a totally monotonous, full-time job. Ida Hoos argues that, in this respect, the office has fared poorly as compared with the automated plant.

> Automation in the factory by and large has been said to enhance intrinsic interest in the job by integrating functions. . . . Automation in the office, by direct contrast, has served to splinter job content into minute, highly repetitive units which can be processed by the computer.[8]

Hoos foresees diminishing worker satisfaction and an increasing contribution to a state of *anomie,* as originally described by

---

8. Hoos, *op. cit.,* p. 125.

Durkheim. Even in the supposedly more favorably affected areas of factory automation, there is little evidence to assume that upgrading will be the general rule. Bright finds no justification for such an assumption.

On the whole, it can be said that it *is by no means certain that automation will shift the work force into higher skills through new specialist jobs or increased percentage of maintenance jobs.* . . . there is a strong possibility of lowering skill requirements and shortening the training period on many operating jobs.[9]

Although the issue of upgrading or downgrading was not investigated in any detail for this study, the writer could not help but form some impressions from visits to automated banks and interviews with officers and consultants. It appears that automation introduced a number of new, higher-skill jobs at the lower hierarchical levels of bank operating personnel. The programmer and the console operator are typical additions of this kind, but they constitute an extremely small number of jobs in most banks. For the vast majority of affected employees, however, automation has done little, if anything, to upgrade jobs or the skill levels required for their performance. To the extent that white-collar work is considered higher-status employment, the advent of the "paper factory" may well be perceived as a downgrading of bank clerical jobs.

7.2. Organizational Structure

The impact of automation on banks' formal organizational structure has, to date, been conspicuous by its relative absence. The response of Merchants Midwest Bank, cited in Chapter III, is typical of most banks questioned: "We have made no organizational changes in introducing automation, nor do we plan any in the immediate future." Most medium-size banks report no

---

9. Bright, *Automation and Management,* p. 197. Italics by Bright.

formal changes in structure either during the conversion stage or as a direct result of it. Senior operations officers have typically taken charge of the conversion and have retained operating responsibility for the computer installation. Where automation committees were formed, they were primarily advisory and educational in nature, their main function being one of keeping department heads posted on plans and progress.

In larger banks, the introduction of automation was often accompanied by the establishment or expansion of staff departments or sections. Titles such as "automation planning," "automated systems" or "systems planning" are typical and serve to describe the department's principal function. Responsibility for the routine operation of computer systems, once installed, was generally left to the existing operations department. Only relatively minor changes, at the lowest hierarchical levels, were generally made in the "line" organizations. These were primarily minor modifications needed to reflect the elimination of bookkeeping departments and the addition of computer operating personnel.

Perhaps the most radical organizational changes that the writer is aware of are found in the two banks discussed in the preceding chapter. Metropolitan Bank's consolidation of all operations in a single major department was probably the most comprehensive and high-level organization change announced by any bank by the mid-1960's. It represents a distinct step towards centralization made possible through automation. On the other hand, the launching of the Automated Services Center of New England by Manufacturers National is an example of significant decentralization, also made possible by automation.

Whether centralization or decentralization will accompany office automation is still widely debated in the literature. Ida Hoos, for example, concludes that "the development of automated data-processing has reversed the trend towards decentralization in many firms."[10] Anshen also concludes that, on balance,

10. Hoos, *op. cit.*, p. 88.

"the marked trend toward decentralization of decision-making in large organizations probably will be slowed and in part reversed."[11] He is quick to add, however, that changes in organizational structure depend on the *purposes* of automation. If decentralization were instituted primarily to place responsibility where the relevant information was available, modern data-processing can readily remove this constraint. On the other hand, "centralized data processing—designed to take advantage of the economics of computer hardware—does not necessarily remove the possibility of returning the computer's output to managers in field locations for their administrative use."[12]

Our findings, both empirical and conceptual, tend to support Anshen's argument. It is management's intent and purpose in exploitation that shape the impact of a basically "neutral" technology. Exploitation at level I, particularly at its lower ranges, need have little or no effect on organizational structure. At this level, it will be recalled, existing services are performed with but little change in work or information flows. As most automated banks are presently in this stage of exploitation, it is not surprising, therefore, that organizational changes are conspicuous by their absence. At the upper ranges of level I, work and information flows may be substantially altered, making modifications in the authority structure possible. Management may elect to make such modifications toward greater·centralization, as in the case of Metropolitan. It may move toward increased decentralization (Essex County, for example) or leave the authority patterns unchanged (as in Fidelity Bank).

Exploitation at level II confronts management with a somewhat different set of conditions. The launching of new services inevitably focuses attention on problems of pricing, merchandising, and selling, as noted in Chapter IV. At the lower ranges of level II very minor organizational changes can successfully cope with these problems. Metropolitan, for example, channelled sales through branch managers, with some assistance from an

---

11. Anshen, *op. cit.,* p. 80.
12. *Ibid.,* p. 81.

advisory staff group. Fidelity transferred a few technical experts into its business development unit. As the level of exploitation rises, however, more drastic organizational changes should be anticipated. Manufacturers National, for example, found it advisable to establish its relatively autonomous Automated Services Center and give it wide latitude in pursuing and promoting sales.

As exploitation reaches progressively higher ranges, at both level I and II, the need for systems and other technical specialists rises. It would be reasonable to expect some additions to staff departments, particularly in the larger banks. Truly radical changes in organizational structure, however, need not be anticipated until exploitation-paths make substantial penetrations into level III. Whether one accepts the March and Simon view of organizations as "congealed decision-making processes."[13] there is little doubt that organizational form is to a large extent determined by its decision-making structure. Anshen states this view clearly and concisely.

Organization structure and administrative process—which define management hierarchy, relationships, and performance—are largely a response to the requirements of decision-making and decision implementation, not to those of manufacturing technology.[14]

It is only at level III that the decision-making capability of automation is effectively exploited. Only at this level of exploitation may we anticipate major changes in the decision-making process and, hence, in organizational structure. This is also the level of exploitation implicitly assumed in predictions of the coming "management revolution" and the sweeping organizational changes in the wake of automation. What form these dramatic changes will take is, at this stage, purely speculative. The exploitation of automation at level III—at least in the commercial banking system—is so limited as to be insignificant.

Experiences observed to date, as well as our conceptual analysis, suggest that a single, optimal organization pattern is not

13. James G. March and Herbert A. Simon, *Organizations* (New York: John Wiley & Sons, Inc., 1958).

14. Anshen, *op. cit.,* p. 66.

likely to emerge. It seems reasonable to assume that different organization impacts will result from level-III exploitation in pursuit of the cost-reducing, as against the revenue-producing, capability. It is even more certain that the shape and evolution of each firm's entire exploitation-path will determine its organizational responses, not merely the latest penetration of the level-III capability. Organization structure, in other words, reflects not only "where we are," but also "how we got here." It is also a product of the combined impacts of the four areas examined in this chapter and their interrelationship.

7.3. Managerial Functions

At the lower hierarchical levels, perhaps the most evident impact of automation has been the "professionalization" of management. The supervision and control of automated bank departments demands new skills and technical understanding. No longer are seniority and long-time familiarity with departmental procedures sufficient qualifications for first-line supervisors. Even at the lowest ranges of level-I exploitation, the supervisor must be able to cope with factory-like operating conditions. Work flows must be closely scheduled and balanced, operator outputs watched, tight deadlines met, and the capabilities and limitations of complex hardware must be thoroughly understood.

As the level of exploitation rises, the demands on the supervisor increase. Greater emphasis is placed on systems-analysis skills and training. For this reason, in most of the banks interviewed there is a tendency to divorce the *design* of new systems from their routine operation. Staff officers are charged with the former so that line supervisors can devote full attention to the latter. This arrangement was noted in three of the four cases reviewed earlier. In all these cases there was similarity in the respective backgrounds of the staff and line officers. Staff departments were wholly, or mostly, recruited from outside the banking system, whereas most line officers had a banking background. Essex County's experience with several line supervisors suggests that a banking background becomes more important as the emphasis on cost-reducing applications becomes greater.

With level-II exploitation, the bank's need for officers with an external orientation rises. Selling officers must be technically trained, or technicians must be taught the selling function. Metropolitan adopted the former approach, Manufacturers National the latter, and Fidelity a combination of both. In one form or another, level-II exploitation results in a modified managerial function: the technical salesman. As relatively few banks exploit this level of capability to any extensive degree at present, it is too early to generalize on the form this new function will take.

One common impact on all officers directly associated with automation is already evident—whether automation is exploited at level I or level II. Automation provides a distinct rise in status. Once a second-class citizen in most banks, the operations officer is now gaining stature. In some banks tangible evidence, in the form of salary and title, attest to this rise. In others it is only reflected in opinions given in interviews. Almost every operations officer and the majority of credit officers interviewed by the writer felt that the status of operations and its personnel had risen with the advent of the computer. At least two banks reported that recruitment of operations officers among college graduates has been greatly stepped up in the past year or two. The higher standing of operations, coupled with greater promotion opportunities in this field, are generally credited with attracting new recruits. Our observations, however, fall somewhat short of the charismatic qualities Ida Hoos attaches to the "new office elite."

Because these men are intimately associated with the "giant brain" which possesses marvelous powers, they themselves are generally regarded by other sectors of the office force as being endowed with magical qualities.[15]

The discussion of changes in managerial functions has focused on operations and staff officers directly associated with the new technology. What of the executives in other banking functions?

---

15. Hoos, *op. cit.*, p. 18.

They have been almost totally unaffected by automation. Some reports or summaries they rely on may be changed in format or frequency, but no major changes in their pattern of operations is yet evident. Many feel that they would like to learn more about computers and their capabilities, but they do not feel this knowledge is an essential prerequisite in the performance of their job. Senior management officers, in particular, foresee a growing need for greater understanding of the computer in the future. This need is probably not too pressing at present levels of exploitation, but will undoubtedly grow in urgency as level-III capabilities are exploited.

It this respect our conceptual reasoning firmly supports Anshen's conclusions.

. . . the critical factor is the purpose served by automation. Mechanizing clerical routines [level I in our terms] creates one situation; mechanizing the decision function [our level III] creates another. Only in the latter situation will there be any important impact on what managers do and how they do it.[16]

7.4. Banking Services

Commercial banks, like any profit-seeking business enterprise, have modified and adapted their repertoire of services over the years. Some of the more recent adaptations were reviewed in Chapter II. The computer presents the automated bank with an almost unlimited range of potential services to choose from. An overview of the diversity of computer applications, already installed or in the planning stage was presented in Chapter IV. An even broader range of possible services opens up if banks are to see themselves—as the president of Manufacturers National suggests—as experts in symbol manipulation and data-processing. In this view symbols need not be restricted to dollar signs, and data-processing need have no relation to money.

16. Anshen, *op. cit.,* p. 80.

Considerable variation in bankers' attitudes as to what constitutes proper or desirable banking services is evident at present. The capacity to broaden services almost indefinitely is, however, clearly exploitable. The experience of Manufacturers National, and the proposed legislation to restrict banking services tightly, bear eloquent testimony to this capability. In our conceptual scheme, it is represented by level-II exploitation. The relationship between exploitation of progressively higher ranges of this level and the expansion of the range of banking services is too obvious to require any elaboration.

It is highly probable that as exploitation-paths are extended we will witness an ever wider range of services performed by the commercial banking system. This will bring banks into competition with other service businesses but will also lead to closer relationships with many of their depositors. A form of subcontracting may well shift entire phases of record-keeping or bookkeeping operations from the depositor's premises to the bank's. The complete payroll services performed by some banks are an early indication of this trend. These services also point up the exciting potential inherent in the interchange of information, between the bank and its customer, in machine-readable form. The exchange of magnetic tapes or even direct communication between computer systems would not only eliminate mountains of paper work, but could also dramatically alter the servicing function of the bank.

The commercial bank's trust department is another area highly suited to expanded computer applications. Considerable advances in investment planning and optimizing portfolio mixes are clearly indicated. Furthermore the banking system's expanded range of services need not be aimed at the corporate depositor solely. A recent tongue-in-cheek *Fortune* article described a miniature computer, TWITCH (The Warning Impulse Timing and Computing Haversack).[17] This versatile gadget,

17. John Slate, "The Warning Impulse Timing and Computing Haversack (TWITCH)," in *Fortune,* Vol. LXIX, No. 5 (May 1964), p. 157.

strapped on the back of each consumer, is visualized as an electronic, all-purpose "tickler." It can remind its wearer of each automobile-loan installment, computes his income-tax liabilities, alerts him to impending birthdays, anniversaries, and insurance-premium payments, and performs a host of other services. This reader, for one, was struck by the long list of personal services (despite the humorous treatment in the article) that an aggressive bank could well offer its depositors.

7.5. The Impacts of Automation— An Oversimplification

In the preceding section we addressed ourselves to the first question posed at the beginning of this chapter. We reviewed the observable impacts of bank automation in four important areas of business activity and related them to the conceptual view of the process of automation. Using this review we can now consider the second question posed earlier. Just how meaningful is any discussion of the topic, the impacts of automation, even if the discussion is confined to a relatively homogeneous industry? The very phrase makes a sweeping, if not obvious, basic assumption. It assumes that automation may be treated as a single, one-dimensional variable. In mathematical terms, the dependent variables—impacts on employment, organization, and so forth—are viewed as a function of the single independent variable—automation. How valid is this implicit assumption?

In the conceptual view of the process of automation, presented in Chapter V, we perceived *automation* as a bundle of capabilities. We argued that a meaningful analysis of the process must recognize at least three significant dimensions of capability. The case experiences cited in Chapter VI and the discussion of their impacts in this chapter point up the close relationship between impacts and the exploitation-path. The exploitation of each dimension and level of capability was seen to result in a different set of impacts. As far as employment is concerned, for example, diametrically opposite impacts result from the pursuit of cost-reducing, level-I capabilities, as compared with revenue-producing, level-II exploitation. The impacts of automation on each firm, therefore, will depend upon the particular mixture of capabilities that it exploits.

As the automation of an industry is actually accomplished by the individual actions of member firms, is it reasonable to anticipate a relatively uniform exploitation mix? This is a restatement of a question we pondered earlier. Can it be reasonably anticipated that all firms in the industry will trace the same or highly similar exploitation-paths? The answer given earlier was a qualified "no." Basic similarities may be expected in the early stages of the path, followed by very marked divergencies.

In the light of this analysis, any discussion of a normal or typical set of impacts on all firms in an industry, must prove grossly oversimplified and inaccurate. Any firm attempting to predict the impacts on its operations from the experiences of another will first have to make sure of basic similarities in their exploitation-paths.

These conclusions bring us back to Bright's findings, with which this chapter opened. "The net impact of automation on a plan or even an industry cannot be derived reliably from a generality. No one kind of experience . . . is a certainty." Our conclusions are even more narrowly drawn. Whereas Bright's observations were based on relatively heterogeneous definitions of both *industry* and *automation,* ours are highly homogeneous, as defined by "commercial banking" and "digital computers."

Using this conclusion, we can now consider the last question posed earlier in this chapter. How valid are any industry-wide or nationwide generalizations about the impacts of automation? Such generalizations are commonly grounded in one of two approaches.

The first, an inductive one, reasons out the probable impacts of the set of technological, economic, and social characteristics inherent in automation. This approach, either explicitly—or, all too often, implicitly—assumes a uniform pattern of exploitation of the capabilities of automation by all firms in the industry. Underlying this assumption is a belief in an optimal mix of capabilities toward which all firms' exploitation-paths will converge. This is a concept similar to the notion of equilibrium in economic analysis. The validity of this assumption is highly debatable. Our analysis of the determinants of the shape of each firm's exploitation-path, in Chapter V, strongly refutes the existence of an optimal path for all firms in the industry.

The second, and presumably less speculative, approach to generalizations is the deductive one. Empirical sample data is analyzed, and the conclusions are generalized to apply to a larger universe. Implicit in this approach is the existence of something akin to Alfred Marshall's "representative firm." It is as well then to recall the number of qualifications to which Marshall's definition is subject.

But our representative firm must be one which has had a *fairly long* life, and *fair* success, which is managed with *normal* ability, and which has *normal* access to the economies, external and internal, . . . account being taken of the *class of goods* produced, the *conditions of marketing* them and the *economic environment generally*.[18]

If generalizations deduced by this method are to be valid, the sample selected for study must be truly representative, not random.

The broad similarity of exploitation-paths in the early phases of automation would tend to make almost every firm selected appear representative. Many—probably most—automated banks are presently in that early stage of tracing their paths. A random sampling of current exploitation-paths will prove overwhelmingly biased in its pattern of exploitation. It is significant that most generalizations currently being propounded about the impacts of bank automation are based almost exclusively on its cost-reducing, level-I capability.

---

18. Alfred Marshall, *Principles of Economics* (New York: The Macmillan Company, 1948), p. 317. Italics are this author's.

The assumption of continuing similarities in exploitation-path patterns is extremely tenuous. Even more questionable is the assumption of a smooth continuity of trend inherent in such projections. Our analysis, on the contrary, strongly suggests marked discontinuities in the process and impacts of automation. The successive penetration of higher levels of exploitation represents a series of discontinuous steps. A shift from level I to level II, for example, implies a change in the bank's relationship with its customers, its perceived service function, its market, and its competitors. A shift to level III alters the pattern of decision-making within the bank and may have radical impacts on its organizational structure and on the functions of its managers. Thus, even if we cannot draw clear-cut lines of demarcation between each level of exploitation, we *can* expect that decisive penetrations of each level will be accompanied by significant discontinuities—even reversals—in impact trends. The risk associated with the trajectory or trend projections from present impacts is self-evident. The reliability of future predictions from current observations thus becomes increasingly questionable as exploitation-paths are extended—particularly as higher levels of capability are exploited.

Even the relatively minor penetrations of the higher capability levels, evident in the four case histories, shows significant discontinuities in impact patterns. A marked, discrete rise in productivity accompanied Essex County's level-III exploitation of the cost-reducing capability. Similarly, a significant change in the orientation of its marketing effort accompanied Manufacturers National pursuit of revenue-producing, level-II exploitation. There seems little doubt that the truly revolutionary impacts of automation (in a variety of manifestations) predicted by many observers, are yet to come—and will come only when decisive penetrations of level III are achieved.

It is for this reason that current forecasts of the impacts of automation—even if based on well-documented empirical evidence—should be viewed with extreme caution and reserve. We

1 4 8

need a more complex conceptual framework than the simple equation of the new technology with its hardware if the process of automation and its impacts are to be better understood. This study attempts to develop one approach toward a more meaningful conceptual framework.

VIII

Implications

This concluding chapter seeks to generalize our findings in two ways: first, a backward look briefly highlighting those conclusions drawn from our case study that have broad relevance to automation in general; and second, a forward look at the implications of our conceptual analysis as a step toward greater understanding of automation and its impacts.

8.1. Summary and Conclusions

Perhaps the most important conclusion to be drawn from the preceding analysis centers on the basic framework within which automation is to be viewed. We tend to visualize automation, almost invariably and intuitively, solely in terms of its hardware. A plant or an office is *automated* when it installs machinery or equipment of a given level of technological sophistication. When bigger, faster, or more complex machinery is installed, the firm becomes *more* automated.

Our analysis clearly suggests that this gross concept of automation is not an adequate analytical tool. Even in an homogeneous industry, employing a highly standardized technology, it fails to explain the significant variations in individual firms' experiences. It becomes even less helpful if applied across in-

150

dustry lines and when stretched to embrace a variety of technological advances.

In the model presented here we still, of necessity, recognize the relationship between automation and its hardware. We depart from the conventional view, however, in two important respects. First, in our model attention is focused not on the technological, but on the operational, capabilities of the hardware. Second, we distinguish between the absolute (or potential) capabilities of the equipment and those actually exploited by the firm. This simply points up the fact that there is a substantial difference in the use to which the same log-log slide rule is put by a college freshman or a skilled engineer.

Hardware capability, in our model, was viewed along three dimensions: cost-reducing, revenue-producing, and level of operation. The first two are closely related to the firm's major economic goals. The third defines the type of function performed. Somewhat arbitrarily, these functions are classified into three operational levels: level I—the performance of functions already undertaken by the firm; level II—the performance of new functions, not formerly included in the firm's repertoire; level III—the performance of decision-making or managerial functions in directing the operations of the firm.

As the equipment is put to use in a successive series of applications, each of its three capability dimensions is exploited to a differing degree. The process of automation can, therefore, be represented by what we have termed the "exploitation-path"—a dynamic record of the extent and sequence of exploitation of each of the three capabilities of automation. This somewhat more elaborate view of the process of automation readily accounts for the empirically observed differences and variations in firms' experiences. No longer need we expect an almost identical set of developments in all firms embracing the same technological advance.

The shape of the exploitation-path traced by each firm is governed by a broad set of environmental and internal determinants. The process of automation in any firm or industry must therefore be analyzed within several, interacting parameters. The technological characteristics of automation represent only one such parameter—and a relatively minor one at that. Our case study indicates that several structural and institutional factors play a major role in shaping and directing the process of automation. We have attempted to identify these factors in Chapter V and, as far as possible, generalize their application beyond our case study of the banking system. We need only list five major determinants to indicate their general application: (1) market structure—as reflected in interindustry and intraindustry competition, as well as cooperation; (2) institutional changes—in the form of shifts in consumer demand, purchasing habits, and legislation; (3) diffusion of technological know-how, by equipment manufacturers, consultants, and the popular press; (4) firm size; and (5) firm location.

It should be noted that the total effect of these determinants cannot be defined by any wholly objective scale. Rather, it is based on each firm's subjective evaluation of each determinant, as it is perceived through its own policies, traditions, and decision-makers. The historical trend that brings automation to any industry tends to provide some uniformity of perception in the early stages of the process. The determinants that first attract the industry's attention to the technological advance reflect a set of acute and unmistakable pressures on most firms in the industry. Their initial response, in the form of adopting automation, is thus likely to be relatively uniform. As the process continues, however, individual perception of the determinants becomes less universal. Local and specialized differences tend to be emphasized, and the process assumes an increasingly individual form in each automated firm.

The banking system's experience with automation is too short-lived to warrant any definitive conclusions. There are strong indications, however, that as the process of automation continues, a number of rather distinct typologies will emerge. Combinations of similar determinants can be expected to lead a group of managements to exploit a relatively uniform mixture of the cost-reducing and revenue-producing capabilities of automation at comparable levels of operation. If this happens, a small number of basic types of exploitation-paths will serve to describe the process of automation within an industry. Even the limited evidence available to date, however, categorically rejects the notion that a *single* path may be viewed as representative or even normative.

Finally, our study confirms what is perhaps obvious. The impacts of automation are directly related to its process. The exploitation of each dimension and level of automation is associated with a distinctive set of impacts. This conclusion not only is logically deduced from our conceptual model but is also confirmed by empirical observation. Even at this early stage of bank automation, the four case histories presented reveal significant variations in impacts. In some areas the variation is only one of degree; in others it is one of direction. The impact of automation on employment, for example, has—at least to date—been uniformly in the direction of fewer job openings in automated banks. In some banks the contraction has been far more pronounced than in others. On the other hand, the impact of automation on the centralization of organizational authority shows diametrically opposite results. Centralization has been increased in some firms, decreased in others but left unchanged in most. In fact, the limited experience observable in bank automation to date suggests that centralization may be increased in some functions and reduced in others, even within the same firm.

With the impacts of automation in any firm directly related to the shape of its exploitation-path, it follows that any discussion of a single set of industry- or economy-wide impacts, of necessity, represents a gross oversimplification. At best, one might expect to discover a series of rather distinct impact patterns, corresponding to the basic types of exploitation-paths identified. Meaningful projections and aggregations can only be developed if due allowance is made for the several basic exploitation patterns that characterize the process of automation.

8.2. Emerging Implications

Our multidimensional view of the process of automation, initially suggests two fundamental generalizations. (1) Once successfully adopted by any industry, automation will rapidly proliferate through it, in response to a broad spectrum of environmental determinants. The more competitive, homogeneous, or interdependent the industry, the more rapid a diffusion rate should be expected. (2) An equally powerful set of determinants assures progressively more intensive exploitation of automation within each individual firm. Once the new technology is adopted, its utilization is not likely to be limited to its initial applications. A growing repertoire of applications, probably of rising complexity, will tend to develop within each automated firm. The directions and levels of exploitation, however, are likely to vary considerably between firms.

The more specific implications of our model are, perhaps, best discussed in three stages, corresponding to the three levels of exploitation.

Level-I exploitation makes use of automation's capacity to improve the performance of traditional firm operations and functions. To a large extent it represents the familiar economic concept of factor substitution. At its lowest ranges it consists of highly conventional mechanization. Machines are substituted for manual labor. Higher-performance machines replace less efficient equipment. Exploitation at the upper ranges of level I is also closely comparable to earlier forms of mechanization. Methods of processing, work flows, and product design are modified and adapted to take full advantage of the new technology. Thus, the process of automation and its impacts at this level can be reasonably expected to parallel earlier experiences with mechanization.

This is confirmed by our case study. Growing task specialization, increased rationalization of process and work flow, standardization of inputs and outputs—all these are clear trends. The growing similarity between factory and office has already been noted. In a sense, both the advantages and the problems characteristic of the manufacturing plant become increasingly applicable to the automated office. Repetitive tasks are more efficiently performed but at the price of greater job monotony. Little or no upgrading is evident in the vast majority of office jobs, although a number of higher-skill openings generally appear in the specialist or technician classification. Increased professionalization of first-line supervision and a tendency to evaluate performance by output is also clearly discernible at this stage.

Our model distinguishes two directions in which level-I capability may be exploited. Ongoing operations can be improved in terms of either lowered cost or increased revenues. This distinction is also present with conventional mechanization. Machines are not used exclusively for the purpose of reducing manufacturing costs. They may often increase sales revenue *directly,* for example, by enhancing product quality or precision. Quite obviously mechanization often increases revenues *indirectly,* via its cost-reducing capability, when the latter is reflected in reduced prices for price-elastic products.

In both mechanization and office automation, the cost-reducing dimension appears to receive greater attention, at least initially. If for no other reason, it is more susceptible to calculation and projection with a reasonably low degree of uncertainty. By contrast, such intangibles as higher quality or more prompt service do not as readily lend themselves to quantification and computation. Similarly, the forecasting of revenues must cope with consumer demand, competitive responses, and other factors outside the direct control of the firm's management. Cost reduction, on the other hand, primarily involves the manipulation of factors largely subject to management control.

Our study suggests that level-I exploitation is likely to direct office automation along paths quite similar to those traced by industrial mechanization. Office automation, in fact, seems peculiarly susceptible to rational evaluation. At the time of writing in 1964 there is practically no evidence of the massive and organized resistance to change that accompanied industrial mechanization. There are as yet no white-collar Luddites.

Level-II exploitation presents a somewhat different picture. At this level, it will be recalled, automation enables the firm to expand its "product line" by the initiation of new services to its clientele. Mechanization has, of course, displayed the same capability in both the product and services area, but to a more limited extent. Conventional advances in mechanization generally lead the firm into new products or services closely related to its traditional area of specialization. Office automation, by contrast, may be viewed as a specialization in data or symbol manipulation—an extremely broad area, cutting across most conventional product, service, or industry classifications. For the firm prepared to interpret its specialty in these terms the range of options is virtually unlimited.

In the terms of our model there is considerable precedent for the exploitation of the lower ranges of level II—new products or services rather closely related to the firm's traditional line. Office automation, however, opens up relatively unexplored areas when exploited at the upper ranges of level II. At these ranges a firm may expand its activities into radically new and different markets and functions. The example of a commercial bank performing engineering calculations for a construction company is a case in point.

By virtue of this extreme flexibility, exploitation at level II is subject to more complex considerations than purely internal economics. The structure of the market in which the firm already participates, as well as the market it seeks to penetrate, become determinants of primary importance. Equally significant are the constraints on the firm's freedom to enter new markets. These may be both internally and externally imposed. A firm's perception of its "proper" function, its comparative advantages, and its public image, are internally imposed. Legislation, in the form of the proposed Multer Bill is an example of an externally imposed constraint.

At this level of exploitation, therefore, considerable variation between individual firms may be anticipated and is in fact already evident. Some firms determinedly exploit level-II applications to the highest range possible, in search of added revenues. Some deliberately restrict the levels of exploitation to highly traditional areas. Others exploit this capability with genuine reluctance. They view it not as a desirable source of revenue but as a defensive measure designed to protect their competitive standing in the market for their principal line of services. Consequently, considerable diversity must be anticipated in the impacts of automation, when exploited at level II.

Organizational structure and the functions of selling executives are directly affected by the firm's entry into new markets. New patterns of merchandising and competing must be developed. Technical skills and familiarity with new industries and their operations must be acquired. Total company resources must be allocated between the demands of the newly expanded and the traditional line of services.

The impact on employment will tend to offset the reduced job opportunities associated with level-I exploitation. The greater the degree of level-II exploitation, the broader the employment opportunities *within the firm*. Whether these will lead to a net increase in *national* employment levels, however, still remains to be seen. Most of the new services currently offered by the banks comprising our case study are sold on their cost-saving advantage to the customer. A given quantity of work is transferred from the customer's organization into the servicing firm's. The transfer is presumably accomplished with a net reduction in the demand for labor, since cost-savings are claimed as its result. This does not rule out the theoretical possibility of accelerated growth of the customer's organization which is made possible by the more efficient supporting services it can draw upon. Hence, there would be an increase in total employment. The latter effect, however, must be viewed as a long-run, second-generation impact of automation. Its short-run, direct impact appears to reinforce the two major economic trends characteristic of recent decades: fewer people are needed to produce a given output of goods and services, and there is a marked shift in new employment opportunities from the goods-producing to the service industries.

In this broader framework, office automation may have one of its most significant impacts on the functions and orientation of the automated firm. Exploitation at level II classifies the firm as a service organization, in addition to its established classification as a bank, an insurance company, or even a manufacturer of ball bearings. As such, it accelerates the current trend toward "contracting out" the many supporting services demanded by American industry. The automated office thus joins a growing segment of the economy specializing in the servicing of other businesses. Its clientele can reap the benefits of specialization based on economies of scale, high-performance capital equipment, and high levels of skill and technical know-how.

The automated office, as a services specialist, possesses the technical characteristics for an even more striking impact on overall employment levels. The "farming out" of data-processing often achieves greater labor savings than are accounted for by specialization alone. Considerable amounts of clerical work can be eliminated altogether. The production of manual records, their transcription to machine language, and the several paper exchanges inherent in many transactions can often be dispensed with, or drastically reduced.

Consider, for example, the net reduction in total clerical work —by both bank and employer—inherent in magnetic-tape processing of an industrial payroll. The bookkeeping entries and balance computations for both employer and bank are disposed of in the same operation. Even more impressive savings in manual clerical records are being made possible by recent advances in data-transmission technology and facilities. The direct communication between computers in the serviced and servicing organizations will eliminate the tedious, costly, and painfully slow manual interstices linking the two systems. The net result is not only a reduction in total demand for clerical labor but also some blurring of the clear-cut boundaries between the functions performed by each firm. Greater interdependence and standardization in interfirm operations should be anticipated. These will, in turn, encourage further organizational restructuring within both servicing and client firms.

Level-III exploitation must, of necessity, be discussed in even more speculative terms. The managerial decision-making capability of automation is only just beginning to be tapped. There is no longer any doubt that computers can successfully deal with extremely complex programmed decisions. Herbert Simon and others make a persuasive case for the computer's ability to cope with "heuristic" or poorly structured problem-solving.[1] Current exploitation of this capability in active business operations, however, is extremely rare and is limited to the lowest ranges of this level. Any discussion of impacts at level III must therefore be recognized as deductive and speculative.

It is at this level of exploitation that automation introduces a new capability, not present in the more conventional forms of mechanization. It is the capability to *direct,* as well as perform, to *manage,* as well as process, the operations of the firm, *all with the same hardware configurations.* There have, of course, been many important advances in the art or science of management. They were not, however, the direct outcomes of technological advances in the basic processing machinery employed by the firm. In office automation, on the other hand, the capability for improved management is part of the total bundle of capabilities embodied in the production machinery. Therefore, it can be exploited at comparatively low incremental costs. The substantial investment in hardware, training, technical skills, and technological sophistication is largely "written off" against level-I and level-II applications. Exploitation at level III is thus constrained more by limitations in knowledge and ingenuity than by capital budgeting restrictions.

Massive efforts are presently being applied to the lifting of this critical limitation by advancing the frontiers of knowledge. Large computer users are not the only active explorers. Because

1. Cf., Simon, *op. cit.,* p. 21.

of the close link between managerial decision-making and mass-produced hardware, the computer manufacturer has become an active missionary for improved management. The resources of a vigorous, sophisticated, multimillion-dollar industry are now enlisted in the research and development of management theory and practice. The advances achieved are made available to a growing number of computer users, most of whom could not afford the huge investments required. An early—and relatively primitive—example of this contribution is represented by the prepackaged portfolio-selection programs developed by the computer manufacturers. A form of management consulting service is, in effect, built into the hardware-and-systems package adopted by the automated firm.

Office automation can, therefore, be expected to herald significant changes in management practice. Such changes, because of the factors enumerated, are likely to proceed at a more rapid rate than has been experienced previously. They are also likely to become diffused through broader segments of each automating industry. As in the case of level-II exploitation, however, considerable diversity in process and impacts can be anticipated between firms.

Level-III applications tend to intensify impacts in both the cost-reducing and revenue-producing directions. We have already noted the striking cost-savings achieved at Essex County National Bank with but limited exploitation of level-III applications. Similarly impressive results are claimed for a number of planned revenue-producing applications utilizing the computer's decision-making capability. Exploitation along this dimension may be expected to offset the trend toward lower employment, which is characteristic of cost-reducing applications. It is doubtful, however, whether any such offset will prove to be of a comparable order of magnitude. As was noted earlier, level-III applications typically tend to rely on the sophisticated exploitation of the computer's "brainpower," rather than its "brute force" in processing masses of data. Such applications do not, as a rule, create any great demand for manual clerical labor.

The many writers who predict radical impacts of automation on organization structure and managerial functions all assume— either explicitly or implicitly—extensive exploitation at level III. At this level, the firm's decision-making process and structure become directly affected by automation. Our study indicates that two frequently predicted trends have already been proved technically feasible: one, increased centralization, and two, some elimination of middle-management functions. Our study also points out, however, that mere technical feasibility does not assure implementation. Automation simply widens the range of options available to the firm's management.

The essence of our conclusions is to reject the gross concept of automation as a one-dimensional process that can be explained simply in terms of the technological hardware employed. It has been shown that no meaningful generalizations can be developed from this approach. Equally unsatisfying is the argument at the other extreme of the spectrum. This view holds that automation is so diverse a process as to make all generalizations totally invalid. Each case, according to this view, must be treated on its own merits. It is our belief that there exists a middle ground between the two views that justifies further research. A useful theory of automation can be developed by abstracting from the individual case experiences in an effort to identify a generally applicable set of concepts and principles. The three-dimensional model presented here is a first step toward such conceptualization of the process of automation.

Bibliography

American Bankers Association, Bank Management Commission, *Magnetic Ink Character Recognition*. Bank Management Publication 138 (July 21, 1956).
————, *Placement for the Common Machine Language on Checks*. Bank Management Publication 141 (April 1957).
————, *Location and Arrangement of Magnetic Ink Characters for the Common Machine Language on Checks*. Bank Management Publication 142 (January 1958).
————, *Account Numbering and Check Imprinting*. Bank Management Publication 144 (June 1958).
————, *A Progress Report–Mechanization of Check Handling*. Bank Management Publication 146 (July 1958).
————, *The Common Machine Language–Final Specifications and Guides*. Bank Management Publication 147R2, Second Revision (December 1963).
————, *Proceedings, National Automation Conference* (New York, November 1963).
Aldom, Robert S., Purdy, Alan B., Schneider, Robert T., and Whittingham, Harry E., Jr., *Automation in Banking*. New Brunswick, New Jersey: Rutgers University Press, 1963.
Amber, George H., and Amber, Paul S., *Anatomy of Automation*. Englewood Cliffs, New Jersey: Prentice-Hall, Inc., 1962.
Anshen, Melvin, "Managerial Decisions," *Automation and Technological Change*. The American Assembly, Columbia University. Englewood Cliffs, New Jersey: Prentice-Hall, Inc., 1962.
"ASA Adopts MICR Standards," *Banking* (July 1964).
"Banking Turmoil—Conflicts Beset Banks," *Wall Street Journal* (October 4, 1965).
Bright, James R., *Automation and Management*. Boston: Harvard University Press, 1958.
————, "Directions of Technological Change and Some Business Consequences," *Automation and Technological Change*. Columbus, Ohio: Battelle Memorial Institute, 1963.

Bross, Irwin D. J., *Design for Decision*. New York: The Macmillan Company, 1961.

Buckingham, Walter, *Automation, Its Impact on Business and People*. New York: Harper & Brothers, 1961.

Burck, Gilbert, "The Assault on Fortress IBM," *Fortune*, Vol. LXIX, No. 6 (June 1964).

Clark, John Maurice, *Competition as a Dynamic Process*. Washington, D.C.: The Brookings Institution, 1961.

Faunce, William A., Hardin, Einar, and Jacobson, Eugene H., "Automation and the Employee," *The Annals of the American Academy of Political and Social Science*. Vol. 340 (March 1962).

Federal Deposit Insurance Corporation, *Annual Report for 1963* (Washington, D.C.: FDIC, 1964).

General Information Manual: Bank Investment Portfolio. White Plains, New York: International Business Machine Corporation, 1964.

Gregory, Robert H., and Van Horn, Richard L., *Automatic Data-Processing Systems*. Belmont, California: Wadsworth Publishing Company, Inc., 1963.
————, *Business Data Processing and Programming*. Belmont, California: Wadsworth Publishing Company, Inc., 1963.

Hoos, Ida Russakoff, *Automation in the Office*. Washington, D.C.: Public Affairs Press, 1961.

Lerner, Max (ed)., *The Portable Veblen*. New York: The Viking Press, 1961.

March, James G., and Simon, Herbert A., *Organizations*. New York: John Wiley & Sons, Inc., 1958.

Marshall, Alfred, *Principles of Economics*. New York: The Macmillan Company, 1948.

Nadler, Paul S., "What Stunts the Growth of Demand Deposits?" *Banking* (January 1964).

National Association of Bank Auditors and Controllers, *NABAC Research Institute Bulletin*, Vol. 4, No. 1 (July 11, 1963).

Newman, William H., and Summer, Charles E., Jr., *The Process of Management*. Englewood Cliffs, New Jersey: Prentice-Hall, Inc., 1961.

Schumpeter, Joseph A., *The Theory of Economic Development*. (Galaxy Edition) New York: Oxford University Press, 1961.

Sheehan, Robert, "What's Rocking those Rocks, the Banks," *Fortune*, Vol. LXVIII, No. 4 (October 1963).

Simon, Herbert A., *The New Science of Management Decision*. New York: Harper & Row, 1960.

Slate, John, "The Warning Impulse Timing and Computing Haversack," in *Fortune*, Vol. LXIX, No. 5 (May 1964).

"Special Report: New Tool, New World," *Business Week* (February 29, 1964).

Thompson, Victor, *Modern Organization*. New York: Alfred Knopf, 1961.

U.S. Congress, House, Joint Economic Committee, Subcommittee on Economic Stabilization, *Automation and Technological Change*, 84th Cong., October 1955.

U.S. Congress, House, Committee on Education and Labor, Subcommittee on

Unemployment and the Impact of Automation, *Impact of Automation on Employment,* 87th Cong. June 1961.

U.S. Congress, House, 88th Cong. 1st Sess., 1963, H.R. 9548.

U.S. Department of Labor, Bureau of Labor Statistics, *Monthly Labor Review,* Vol. 85, No. 9 (September 1962).

Wiener, Rose, "Changing Manpower Requirements in Banking," *Monthly Labor Review* (September 1962).

Index

Accounting
  demand-deposit, 3, 17, 27, 48,
    67, 69, 73, 85, 87, 99, 133,
    136
  deposit, 38
  general ledger, 115
  loan, 38, 67, 69, 87
  punched-card, 16f
  savings deposit, 38, 85
  services, 70, 71
Accounts
  bank employee, 48
  direct debiting of, 65, 71
  reconciliation of, 121, 126
Accounts receivable, 87
Advertising, 52
Amber, George H., 78
Amber, Paul S., 78
American Bankers Association, 2f,
    23ff, 27, 35, 36, 38, 57, 59,
    62, 72, 99, 100, 101
American Standards Association, 25
Analysis
  profitability, 119
  sales, 115
  systems, 41
  three-dimensional, 81ff, 85
Anatomy of Automation (Amber
    and Amber), 78n

Annual Report for 1963 (FDIC),
    29n
Anomie, 136f
Anshen, Melvin, 82, 139f, 143
Assets, 49, 58, 67, 113, 117, 120,
    124, 129
Association of Data Processing Or-
    ganizations (ADAPSO), 76,
    115
Atomic Energy Commission, 20
Audit, 56ff
Auditors, 71
Authority patterns, 139
Automated Services Center of New
    England, 115, 117, 138, 140
Automatic Data-Processing Systems
    (Gregory and Van Horn),
    32n, 80n
Automatic debiting *see* Checking
    accounts, direct debiting of
Automaticity, order of, 78
Automation
  adaptability, 51
  adoption, parameters of, 6–30
  amount of, 29
  applications, 86, 104, 115, 126,
    152
  applications, "spinning off" of,
    124

1 6 5

Automation (*cont'd*)
assumptions, 145
benefits, 33, 41
built-in delay, 54
capability, 81, 82*f*, 147, 159
case histories, 106–129
characteristics, 146
conceptual view of, 77–105
conclusions about, 150*ff*
contrasts, 106–129
conversion to, 34*f*, 41, 46, 48,
  49*f*, 133, 138
cooperative centers, 45*t*, 55, 56,
  115, 121
cost, 54
cost-reducing capability, 63, 80*f*,
  83, 85*ff*, 100, 104, 107, 109*ff*,
  111, 122, 125, 127, 133*f*, 141,
  148, 151, 159
cost-to-returns calculus, 3, 36,
  40–47, 93
decision to automate, 3, 31–60
defined, 77, 146
demand for, 7
design, 33*f*
direct-reading system, 23, 24
direction taken by, 79
diversity, 161
economic questions, 35*f*
education of management to, 60
employment and, 133
errors in system, 35
evaluation for, 46
experiences with, 51–54, 131
experimentation with, 51, 116
exploitation path of, 4, 85–102,
  104, 105, 109, 110, 111, 114,
  122, 134, 140, 144*f*, 149, 151,
  153
feasibility studies, 2, 32, 35*f*
generalizations about, 131, 146*f*,
  161

hardware, 5, 78, 93, 149, 150*f*,
  159*f*
history of, 19
impact of, 1, 4, 79, 130–149
implementation, 35, 36, 104, 160
levels of, 77*ff*
machine control with, 18
mechanical features, 81
obstacles to proliferation, 54–60
and operating costs, 44*t*, 45*t*
operational level, 79, 81, 82*f*
oversimplification, 145–149
patterns, 106
and personnel, 43, 44*t*, 45*t*
pioneers in, 47*ff*
planning, 46
preparation for, 46
problem-solving with, 18
process of, 77–105, 153
proliferation, 47–54, 61, 154
promotion, 94
purchase of equipment, 46
purposes of, 139
reasons for automating, 37*t*
revenue-producing capability, 81,
  83, 85*ff*, 100, 104, 107, 109*ff*,
  111, 122, 125, 127, 133*f*, 141,
  148, 151, 159
savings from, 40, 54
service bureaus, 55
site preparation, 46
six steps, 85*ff*
sophistication of, 83, 98
standardization, 53
supply of, 7
systems planning, 35
technical characteristics, 92–95
technical questions, 35
three-dimensional model, 81*ff*, 85
timetable for, 33*f*
work flows, 63, 134, 139, 154

see also Computer; Data processing

Automation and Management (Bright), 2*n*, 42*n*, 130*n*, 137*n*

Automation: Its Impact on Business and People (Buckingham), 132*n*

Automation in the Office (Hoos), 64*n*, 132*n*, 136*n*, 138*n*, 142*n*

Automation Survey (ABA), 2, 36*ff*

Balances, offsetting, 73

Bank of America, 21*ff*, 25, 35, 47

Bank Computer Center of Connecticut, 55

Bank Management Commission (ABA), 23, 38

Bankers' attitudes, 144

Banking
  described, 1
  institutional changes in, 91*f*
  "retail," 21, 47, 92, 103
  on "threshold of revolution," 131
  trends in, 15

Banking commissions, state, 7*n*, 12

Banking and Currency, Congressional Committee on, 75*f*

Banks, commercial, 8*t*
  accounting services, 70, 71
  accounts, direct debit of, 65
  accounts, reconciliation of, 82, 121, 126
  activity of, 11, 44
  adoption of computers, 6–30
  advantage of large, 129
  asset management, 127
  assets, 47, 101, 117, 124
  audit, 56*ff*
  automation, amount of, 29
  automation committees, 32
  automation program, 86
  bid preparation, 98

billing and collection, 71

bookkeeping, 15, 67, 86, 87, 96, 136

branches, number of, 12, 91, 113, 117, 119

and cash flow, 10

centralization, 118, 119*f*, 138*f*

changes in, 91*f*

changing trends in, 7–17

charges, 74–119

check-handling, 3, 28, 112

and competition, 8*t*, 13, 64, 90, 92*n*, 95–99, 149

computational services, 72

control, 56*ff*, 68, 109

cooperation, 53, 99*f*

cooperative data center, 45*t*, 55, 56

correspondents, 56, 69, 121

cost-to-returns calculus, 3, 36, 40–47

credit data, 70, 75

customer relations, 46, 65, 66

decentralization, 112, 119, 138*f*

decision-making, 31*f*

decision to automate, 3, 31–60

demand-deposit accounting, 3, 13, 48, 67, 69, 73, 85, 87, 88, 133, 136

departments and divisions, 120

deposits, 29, 30*t*

depreciation allowances, 10

dividend paying, 70

earnings, 10

economic factors, 7–17

expansion, 12

experiences with automation, 106–129, 131

freedom of choice, 66

function, 117

goals, 103

growth, 21

Banks, Commercial (cont'd)
image of, 10, 92
incentive payments, 68, 108, 110
income, 9, 101
independence, 116
and industry, 56, 102
institutional factors, 7–17
interest, 13, 96, 97
investment officers, 89
joint ventures with nonbanks, 56
loans, 9, 10, 13, 38t, 98f
location, 90, 101f
managerial functions, 5
market research, 68f, 70
marketable services, 66
merchandising function, 74
mergers, acquisitions, and consolidations, 12, 119
methods research department, 47
money management, 68f
money, sale of, 117
monetary policy, 7
mortgage financing, 13, 67, 69
New York City, 11, 22
no-layoff policy, 42, 58, 91, 118, 132
number, 12, 30t
operating costs, 13, 36
operating procedures, 32, 38, 117, 119, 138
operations committees, 50
operations research, 72
organizational structure, 4, 137–141
outside servicing by, 55
payroll, 65, 68, 70, 98, 121
personal finance, 95
portfolio selection, 68f, 87, 95, 127
posting, 87
pressures on, 7
product line, 66

profit, 13
"profit center," 115
proof and transit, 16, 67, 110
regulation of, 7, 12, 92
reporting, 42
"retail" function, 10, 21, 47, 92, 103
revenue, 10
selling services, 66, 74
services, 5, 13, 55, 64f, 66, 72ff, 81, 82, 90f, 96, 97f, 107, 113, 126
sharing computers, 55
size, 21, 29, 30t, 44t, 45t, 55, 56, 90, 97, 100f, 106, 122, 137
small, 55, 56, 66, 100, 113, 116
statement mailing, 112, 113
stock transfer, 70
strains on, 11
supervision of automated departments, 141
transactions, volume of, 43, 44t
trusts, 38, 39t, 67f, 144
underwriting, 92, 98, 127
variations in, 5
West Coast, 15
Bay State Computer Center (Waltham, Mass.), 55
Bendix Electronics Corporation, 113
Benefits, tangible and intangible, 33
Billing, 71
Blue Cross, 65, 71
Bond Trade Analysis program (IBM), 94
Bonds, 10, 69, 87, 98
Bookkeeping, 15, 67, 86, 87, 96, 136
double-entry, 68
Booz, Allen & Hamilton, Inc., 2f, 34, 39, 40, 42, 44t, 45t, 102, 132, 133

Branches, bank, 113, 117, 119
  number of, 12, 91
Bright, James R., 2n, 6, 18, 28f,
    42, 77f, 80, 130, 137, 146
Brokers, 71
Bross, I. D. J., 103n
Buckingham, Walter, 132
Budgeting, 120
Burck, Gilbert, 53n
Bureau of the Census, 19
Burroughs Corporation, 25
Business Data Processing and Pro-
    gramming (Gregory and Van
    Horn), 19n, 37n
Business Week, 20

Calculating machines, 37
California, 22
Carrier, in reading, 23
Cash, 67
Central processor see Computer
Centralization, 118, 119f, 138f,
    153, 161
Certified public accountants, 71, 76
Change, 7–17
Charitable institutions, 116
Check Standards Under the Com-
    mon   Machine   Language
    (ABA), 25
Checking accounts, 48, 51, 54, 103
  regular, 38, 44t
  special, 10, 38, 50
Checks
  charges, 74
  direct debiting of, 65, 87
  dividend, 70
  dual-posting, 16
  field locations for code, 24
  handling of, 3, 15ff, 22, 27, 38f
  machine-processing, 28
  posting, 16
  and premiums, 65

  processing, 112
  proving, 16, 38, 39t, 40t, 67, 110
  punched-card, 16f
  racking, 16
  reading, 22, 23
  reconciliation, 82, 121, 126
  redesign, 34
  sorting, 66
  transit, 16, 38t, 39t, 40t, 67, 110
  volume of, 11, 13
Christmas Club accounts, 51
City administration, 116
Clark, John Maurice, 80, 98
Clerical work see Work, clerical
Coding, 24, 26
Collection, 71
Commercial banks see Banks, com-
    mercial
Commercial service bureau, 55
Competition as a Dynamic Process
    (Clark), 80n
Compilers, 94; see also Programs,
    canned
Comptroller of the Currency, 7n
Computer
  adoption, 6–30
  applications, 4, 39t, 40t, 61–76,
      78, 104, 112, 115
    design, testing, and imple-
        menting, 62
    external, 66, 69–72
    factors in diversification, 63–
        72
    internal, 66–69, 126
    number, 62
  auxiliary equipment, 63
  back-up capacity, 63
  capability, 19, 66, 79ff, 81
  central processor, 15
  common language, 23, 26, 27
  corporate trust work, 38
  cost, 20

Computer (*cont'd*)
  as cost saving device, 35*f*, 63
  debugging, 34, 48, 50, 68
  "decision" by, 67, 88, 112, 127, 140
  determinants of use, 4
  development, 19
  direct-reading system, 23, 24
  down time, 41
  experimentation, 19, 47, 48
  general-purpose, 62, 92
  graphic representation of applications, 83*ff*
  hardware, 5, 78, 93, 94, 149
  history, 19
  implementation, 35, 63
  information, 25
  input, 22, 23, 24, 68, 82, 95, 136
  installation, 63
  as instructional tool, 47
  internal applications, 38*t*
  introduction of, 37*f*
  level of mechanization of, 78
  lower cost, 56
  manufacturers of, 33*f*
  mathematical simulation by, 66
  media, 34
  military applications, 20
  nonprogrammed decisions, 83
  obsolescence, 94
  operating staff, cost, 63
  operations, 18
  options in use of, 61–76
  output, 38, 108, 110, 136
  parallel operation, 46, 48, 50
  peripheral equipment, 15, 27, 63
  pioneering efforts, 22
  potential, 59
  program, 20, 34, 46
  programmed decisions, 83
  rental, 63, 64, 94
  run-timing, 41, 94
  scientific and mathematical applications, 20
  shakedown period, 42
  sharing of, 55
  size, 20
  software, 34, 56, 93, 104
  sophistication of, 83, 98, 129, 160
  special-purpose, 20
  speed, 18
  stored program, 20
  systems analysis, 41
  tape, 50, 57
  technical advances, 17–21, 28*ff*
  technical characteristics, 92–95
  see also Automation; Data processing
Congress, 75*f*, 130, 132
Consolidations, 12, 119
Constraints, 156
Consultants, 33, 40, 49, 50, 105, 152
Contracting out, 158
Control, 56*ff*, 68
Control Data Corporation
  GI5 computer, 113
  Model 6600, 20
Cooperative data centers, 45*t*, 55, 56, 115, 121
Corporations, 9*f*
Correspondents, 64, 98, 121
Cost distributions, 115
Cost-versus-returns calculus, 3, 93
Costs, 32, 36, 97
  "after," 33
  "before," 33
  current, 40
  cutting of, 15
  implementation, 35, 44*t*, 45*f*, 63, 93
  manufacturing, 155
  marginal, 63

one-time, 45*f*
operating, 36, 44*t*, 91
payback period, 44*t*, 46, 51, 118
production, 111
programming, 50
"rational," 41
records, 42
reduction, 81, 83, 85*ff*, 97, 100, 104, 107, 111, 122, 125, 127, 133, 140, 146, 148, 151, 155, 157
saving of, 35*f*
tangible, 33
County Trust Company (White Plains, N.Y.), 24
Credit, 70, 75, 96
Credit unions, 8*t*
Customer relations, 46, 65, 98, 99, 116, 121, 126

Dartmouth College, 112
Data processing, 17, 34, 94, 142; *see also* Automation; Computer
of checks, 28
coding, types, 24
common language, 23, 26, 27
corporate trust work, 38
history of, 19
of information, 18, 25
input, 22, 23
media, 34
military applications, 20
scientific and mathematical applications, 20
volume, 91, 94, 119
Debugging, 34, 48, 50, 68
Decentralization, 112, 119, 138*f*
Decision-making, 31*f*, 82*f*, 98, 103, 112, 127, 139, 159*ff*
unanimity in, 104
Demand, consumer, 152

Demand deposits, 3, 9, 13, 17, 21, 22, 27, 39*t*, 40*t*, 48, 50, 62, 63, 67, 69, 73, 85, 87, 99, 118*f*, 133, 136
Department of Justice, 7*n*
Department of Labor, 59, 132
Department stores, 70, 87
Depositors, 64, 92, 98, 144
captive, 65
competition for, 98
new, 65
Deposits, 7, 8*t*, 9, 10, 29, 55, 87; *see also* Demand deposits; Savings deposits
competition for, 9
composition of, 9
turnover, 11
volume, 11
Depreciation, 10
Design for Decision (Bross), 103*n*
Determinants, 89*ff*, 103*ff*, 152, 154
Discontinuities, 148
Dollars, constant, 11
Down time, 41
Durkheim, Émile, 136*f*

Earnings, 10
Economics, 35
Electronic data processing *see* Data processing
Employees
attrition, 133
dehumanization of, 1
downgrading, 137
errors of, 108
morale, 59
no-layoff policy, 42, 58, 91, 118, 132
number, 91, 109, 132
operating duties, 58
production rate, 108, 119
regimentation of, 1

Employees *(cont'd)*
 resistance, 58
 technical training, 142
 training, 46, 104
 turnover, 80, 91, 107*f*, 118, 124, 131
 and unions, 58, 81, 111
 upgrading, 137, 142, 155
 wages, 13, 14*t*, 43, 108, 109, 110
 see also Personnel
Employment, 5, 131–137, 157; *see also* Labor; Personnel
 and automation, 133
 growth, 133
 increase, 135
 quality of, 136
 reduction, 134*f*
Engineering calculations, 115
Environment, 58, 91, 111
Equipment, 52
 auxiliary, 63
 current, 41
 expansion of, 34
 lower-cost, 99
 maintenance and service, 34
 mechanical, 110
 off-line operations, 63
 peripheral, 27
 punched-card, 16*f*, 47, 65
 purchase of, 46
 rental, 63, 64
 requirements, 53
 selection, 33*f*
 specifications, 33
ERMA (Electric Recording Machine Accounting), 21, 22, 25
Essex County National Bank (pseud.), 107–113, 118, 122, 134, 135, 139, 142, 149, 160
Error, 71, 108
Executives, 142; *see also* Management; Officers

Experimentation, 51, 116
Exploitation, 83*ff*, 92, 99, 106
Exploitation, of automation, 4
Exploitation path, 85–102, 104, 105, 109, 110, 111, 114, 122, 134, 140, 144*f*, 149, 151, 153

Factory, 110
Feasibility studies, 2, 32, 34, 35*f*, 40, 43, 44*t*, 50, 52
Federal Bank Service Corporation, 55
Federal Deposit Insurance Corporation, 7*n*, 29*n*, 75
Federal Reserve banks, 7*n*
Federal Reserve System, 25, 57, 75, 99
Fidelity Bank and Trust Company (pseud.), 47*ff*, 51, 64, 124–129, 139*f*, 142
Field locations, 24
Files, 68
Finance companies, 69, 99
Financial institutions, 8*t*
Firm
 changes in, 152
 contributions of, 99
 functions, 131, 143*ff*
 interfirm operation, 158
 location, 152
 managerial responsibility in, 131, 141*ff*, 161
 organizational restructuring, 159
 organizational structure, 131–141, 161
 pressures on, 152
 product line, 156
 representative, 147
First National City Bank (New York), 22*f*, 25, 27, 47
Fixtures, 46
Fluorescent-ink code, 24

Forecasts, 104
Forms, 34
Fortune, 144

General Electric Company, 19
General Information Manual: Bank Investment Portfolio (IBM), 94*n*
Giannini, A. P., 21
Goals, 103
Government regulation, 92
Great Depression, 1
Gregory, Robert H., 18, 19*n*, 32, 37, 52, 57, 80, 81

Hanning, Richard W., 18
Hardin, Einar, 59
Hardware, 5, 93, 149, 150*f*, 159*f*
  capability of, 78
  rental, 94
Hoos, Ida R., 64*n*, 110, 132, 136, 138, 142
Hospitals, 116

Imperial Germany and the Industrial Revolution (Veblen), 54
Incentives, 68, 108, 110
Income, 9, 101
Industry
  and commercial banks, 56
  defined, 146
Information, 25, 37, 52, 100
  flow, 139
  management, 37, 68, 82, 95, 112, 136, 154
  "no secrets" policy, 100
  restriction, 127
Innovation, 28*f*, 80*f*, 126
Input, 22, 23, 24
  punched-card, 19
"Instant money," 96
Insurance companies, 69, 70

Interest, 13, 96, 97
Internal Revenue Service, 59, 70
International Business Machines, 21, 25, 69
  IBM 650, 19, 20, 47*f*
  IBM 1240, 56
  IBM 1401, 50, 94
  IBM 7070, 48
  IBM 7090, 83
International Telephone and Telegraph Corporation, 22, 27
Inventory control, 115
Investments, 69

Jacobson, Eugene H., 59
Jobs, 133, 135*ff*

Kelley, William F., 59
Kley, John A., 24

Labor, shortage of, 1; *see also* Employment; Personnel
Language, common machine, 23, 26, 27, 99, 118
Legislation, 156
Levels of exploitation, 83*ff*, 93, 100, 106, 109*ff*, 122, 129, 134, 139*ff*, 154*ff*
Levels of operation, 77*ff*, 94*ff*, 126, 127, 136, 146, 151
Loans, 10, 38*t*, 39*t*
  business, 13, 38*t*
  consumer, 13, 38*t*
  installment, 39*t*, 40*t*, 50, 51, 67, 69, 87, 95
  mortgage, 38*t*, 67
  short-term, 9
  small, 98*f*
Loss, 44

Machinery, control of, 18
Magnetic-bar code, 24

Magnetic-ink character recognition, 24, 26, 56, 99, 113
Magnetic tape *see* Tape
Management, 1, 32, 33, 35, 37, 38, 46, 69, 73, 98, 103, 111, 112, 125, 139, 159, 161
attitude of, 58*ff*
decision by, 82*f*
information service, 68, 82, 95, 112
information systems, 37, 52
operations, 112
professionalization of, 141
revolution, 140
Managerial capability, 82*f*
Managerial control reports, 115
Manufacturers, 33*f*, 52*f*, 116, 152
competition, 52
contribution, 93, 94, 129
maintenance and service by, 34
Manufacturers National Bank (pseud.), 113–117, 121, 122, 135, 138, 142, 143, 144, 149
March, James G., 140*n*
Market
location, 102
new, 157
potential, 74
research, 68, 70, 74, 98
structure, 152
Market, stock, *see* Stock exchange
Marketing, 121
Massachusetts Institute of Technology, 112
Marshall, Alfred, 147
Mechanization, 81, 87, 110, 134, 154, 155
levels of, 77*ff*
profile, 78
of systems, 37
Media, 34
Merchandising, 157

Merchants Midwest Bank (pseud.), 49*ff*, 52, 137
Mergers, 12, 119
Methods research, 47, 49, 124
Metropolitan Bank and Trust Company (pseud.), 117–124, 126, 135, 138, 139*f*
MICR, 24, 26, 56, 99, 113
Modern Organization (Thompson), 125*n*
Monetary policy, 7
Money, 7
turnover, 12
Money market behavior, 66
Monotony, 136, 155
Mortgage financing, 13, 38*t*, 67, 69
Mortgage servicing companies, 69
Multer, Abraham, 75, 76n, 135, 156
Multiple-listing service, 115
Municipal water systems, 71
Mutual savings banks, 8*t*

Nadler, Paul S., 11*f*
National Association of Bank Auditors and Controllers (NABAC), 108
National Automation Conference (ABA), 2*f*, 57, 72
National Automation Survey (ABA) 36*ff*
National Banking Act (1933), 10
Needs, 45
New England, 107
New Science of Management Decision (Simon), 83*n*
New York Stock Exchange, 42
Newman, William H., 31, 103*n*
Newspapers, 116
Noise, 110

Obsolescence, 94

Office automation, 155*f*, 158*f*, 160
Office Equipment Manufacturers Committee, 24
Officers, 64, 115, 118, 123, 141*f*
  interviews with, 2, 3
  see also Management
"On the Merits of Borrowing" (Veblen), 54
"On the Penalty of Taking the Lead" (Veblen), 54
Operations, high-volume, 117
Operations group, 50, 120
Operations research, 72, 101, 127
Operators, 34, 63, 64, 132, 142
Order of automaticity, 78
Organizations (March and Simon), 147
Output, 38, 108, 110, 119, 136, 154

Paper, commerical, 10
  processing, 11
  volume of, 11, 17
Paper factory, 111, 137
Paperwork, 38, 104, 116, 144
  cost of handling, 103
  volume of, 91, 94, 103, 107, 118, 131
Parallel operation, 46, 50
Passbooks, 86
Payback period, 46, 51
Payroll, 65, 68, 70, 98, 115, 121, 126, 158
Peripheral equipment, 15
Personnel, 32, 49, 91, 101, 107*f*, 118, 124, 131*ff*, 142
  automation and, 43, 44*t*, 45*t*
  costs of, 13
  number, 44*t*
  reductions in, 43
  see also Employees

Posting, 16
  dual, 16
Prepackaged program *see* Programming, canned
Press, 152
Prices, transfer, 115
Pricing, of services, 72*ff*
Principles of Economics (Marshall), 147
Problem, identification of, 31
Problem-solving, 18
Procedures, current operating, 32
Process of Management (Newman and Summer), 31*n*, 103*n*
Processing, 11
Production
  costs, 111
  rate, 108, 110
  scheduling and control, 108
Productivity, 132
  average, 134
Products, cost of, 13
Profit margins, 13, 15
Profitability analysis, 119
Profit-making, 7
Program, 20, 34, 46
  special-purpose, 125
Programmers, 58
Programming, 48, 72
  canned, 50, 53, 94, 99, 105, 128
  costs, 50
  linear, 66
Projections, 41*ff*, 104, 149
Proliferation, 47–60
  horizontal, 61*f*
  vertical, 61
Property assessment, 115
Proving, 16, 67
Public schools, 116
Public utilities *see* Utilities
Punched-card equipment, 16*f*, 19, 47

Racking, 16
Rate *see* Production, rate
Reading, 24, 27
Ready credit, 96
Real estate board, 116
Records, 34, 57, 158
  accounting, 56
  conversion, 46
  tape, 50
Redesign, 34
Remington Rand *see* Sperry Rand
  Corporation
Reporting, 42
Reports, 34, 68, 108, 115, 119
Research, 48, 58, 126*f*, 161
  market, 68, 98
  methods, 124
Restaurants, 116
Return, 36, 54
Revenue, 10, 101, 157
  production of, 81, 83, 85*ff*,
    100*ff*, 107, 114, 122, 127,
    140, 146, 148, 151, 155
Routing, 111
Run-timing, 41

Salaries *see* Wages
Sales analysis, 115
Sales campaigns, 52
Sales, technical, 75
Sampling, 147
Savings, 44, 54, 119, 133
  negative, 43
Savings deposits, 8*t*, 9, 13, 22, 38,
  39*t*
Savings and loan associations, 8*t*
Schumpeter, Joseph, 18, 53
Securities and Exchange Commis-
  sion, 42
Service bureaus, 55, 56, 116
Services, 5, 90, 97*f*, 107, 113, 115,
  126, 143*ff*

costs of, 13
diversification of, 87
external, 69–76
frequency of, 91
improvement of, 81*f*
internal, 67*ff*
marketing of, 74*ff*
new, 81, 82
quality of, 91
personal, 145
pricing of, 74*ff*
sale of, 74
search for, 96
Shakedown period, 42
Shifts, 110
Simon, Herbert A., 83, 140*n*
Slate, John, 144*n*
Slave, in reading, 23
Software, 34, 56, 93, 104
Sorter-reader, 15, 27, 76
Special checking accounts *see*
  Checking accounts, special
Specialists, 140
Sperry Rand Corporation, UNI-
  VAC-1, 19, 20
Standardization, 53, 154
Stanford Research Institute, 21
State banking commissions *see*
  Banking commissions, state
State examiners, 57
Statements, 112*f*
Statistical forecasting, 115
Statistical summaries, 115
Stock exchange, 88
Stockholders, 70
Study team, 32
"Suggested New Services Banks
  Can Offer with Computers"
  (ABA), 62
Summer, Charles E., Jr., 31, 103*n*
Supervisors, 111, 141

Systems
  advanced planning, 117*f*, 120*f*
  analysis, 37, 52
  design, 33*f*, 81, 141
  management information, 37, 52,
    82, 112
  mechanization level, 37, 52
  operation, 141
  redesign, 37
  research, 64
  simplifying, 37
  symbol manipulation, 143

Tabulator, 65
Tape, 50, 57, 70, 158
Task force, 32
Tax collection, 115
Technical Subcommittee on Mechanization of Check Handling
  (ABA), 23*ff*, 27
Technicians, 34
Technology, new, 17–21, 28*f*, 35,
  94
  acceptance of, 53
  adoption of, 31–60
  diffusion of, 152, 154
  economic considerations, 46
  exploitation, 79, 85
  and historical momentum, 90
  investigating, 52
  missionaries of, 64
  proliferation of, 28
  reliability, 51
Telephone answering service, 116
Tellers, 87
Thompson, Victor, 125
"Tickler," 145
Time deposits, 8*t*, 9, 13, 22; *see
  also* Savings deposits
Trade-ins, 34

Training, 46, 49, 51, 53
Transactions, cash and asset, 67
Transfer prices, 115
Transistor, 20
Transit, 16, 67
Treasurer (U.S.), 17
Trusts
  corporate, 39, 40, 70
  personal, 39, 40, 67*f*
TWITCH (The Warning Impulse
  Timing and Computing Haver-
  sack), 144
Type Design Committee (ABA),
  25

Unemployment, 1, 136
Unionism, 58, 91, 111
UNIVAC *see* Sperry Rand Cor-
  poration
Utilities, 71

Valley National Bank (Phoenix),
  26
Values, 92, 103
Van Horn, Richard L., 18, 19*n*,
  32, 37, 52, 57, 80
Variables, 103*f*
Veblen, Thorstein, 54

Wages, 13, 14*t*, 43, 108, 110
Water systems, 71
West Coast, 15, 22
Wiener, Rose, 133
Work, clerical, 37, 43, 80, 86, 110,
  111, 158, 160
Work flows, 63, 134, 139, 154
Work, routing of, 111, 139
World War II, 7, 15, 91, 103

YMCA, 116